CW01647531

NO HALF MEASURES

Burt Rickman

ISBN-13: 978-1-3999-6800-3

Contents

Contributions

The front cover photograph was done by Andrew Ghafoor at Black Dog Fine art Photography.

Introduction

I've thought a lot about how I am going to start this book, but I think I just need to jump right into it. My name is Burt, and I am from Manchester. I am 17 years old at the time of writing this, and I would hazard a guess that I am five foot eight – maybe I'll even be five foot nine when this book is published. I am the oldest brother – I have three younger siblings – which makes mine a family of six. I decided that I wanted to write this book in August 2022, as I wanted to share what it is like living with a disability. In my case, I will be showcasing some of the key things about living with left-side cerebral palsy hemiplegia. I apologise that the start of the book is mainly other people's recollections, but as you can imagine, me being such a young age, I can't remember what exactly happened. The memories may not be 100 per cent factual, but they are as I remember them and how my mum and stepdad remember them. I hope that this book benefits you in some way, but if it doesn't, enjoy reading it anyway.

Birth

I was born in November 2004, nearly two weeks after my expected due date. My mum wanted to have me at home, but that plan quickly went out of the window because she was in labour with me for far too long. In total, my mum was in labour for more than 60 hours and had a terrible experience with the hospital.

It started when she first got into the hospital, and she was allocated a room. At this point, my mum had been in labour for 28 hours, and the doctors decided that she needed an epidural. It took the doctors six or seven attempts to insert the needle, and as they were using a thick guide needle, it caused my mum a lot of pain. There were two other major problems: the theatres were full, and there was another person in front of us in the queue. After about 40 hours of being in labour, the doctors started talking about using the epidural to do a C-section to get me out.

Normally, the doctors do C-sections while the mother is still awake and use a nerve block, so they feel no pain. Local anaesthetics and nerve blocks do not work for my mum. She can't go to the dentist to get a filling because she can still feel the pain. This was why it was important that the theatre was full. If she was going to have a C-section, she would have to be put to sleep first. The doctor who was overseeing what was happening with us decided that my mum was going to have a C-section while awake. My mum pleaded with the doctor not to have that done, but the doctor ignored her. She was prepared and ready for the C-section, and a screen was put up. It was only when my mum started screaming and shouting at the doctor, for fear of being able to feel being cut open, that they took any notice of what she was saying. It was at this point my vitals started dropping. The doctor then used cold spray a few times on my mum’s legs to see whether she was telling the truth. My mum was able to tell the doctor where she felt the spray, and she was right every time. The doctor was shocked, and my mum could see the panic in their face when they realised that she was telling the truth. At this point, my mum had been in labour for 50 hours. As the theatres were full, she gave birth to me naturally. In that time, I had managed to wrap the umbilical cord around my neck. This is not abnormal, as this happens in 20 to 30 per cent of all deliveries. It was only a problem for me because it was wrapped around my neck for so long. It caused a restriction of oxygenated blood to my brain, which led to a part of my brain dying off. This means that I have the symptoms of someone who has had a stroke because it is the same mechanism of injury.

After an intense struggle, I was finally born, and the first thing that happened to me was getting an oxygen mask over my face. I am no expert, but they don't do that with healthy babies. They then wrapped me in a blanket and gave me to my mum. The midwives then kept coming into the room and wrapping me up with an extra blanket because my temperature was dropping. With the symptoms that I was displaying, I should have been put into the baby unit, but I wasn't: I stayed in the same room as my mum. She was worried and chased the midwives up the ward saying that I was not waking up to feed and something was wrong. When me and Mum got home, my mum got into bed and slept for 24 hours solid to recover from what had happened. She only woke up to drink a Lucozade.

From zero to six years old

As many months passed, all seemed well with me until I wasn't hitting milestones at the right age. There were telltale signs that I had something wrong with me. The first clue that Mum noticed was that I was slumping to one side in my highchair. Another clue that she noticed was that I would only eat food with my right hand, even if the food was closer to my left hand. This was because I always kept my left hand shut. These little signs were the start of my mum wondering whether I had a problem. I was also struggling to crawl, as I was not using my left side, and my gran knew I should have been able to do that by eight months old. My gran told my mum that there was something amiss with me and I should be seen by a doctor. As I was my mum's first child, she didn't know when I should have reached certain milestones. My mum agreed with my gran that I had an issue, but my mum thought I didn't need to be checked. However, there must have been some doubt in her mind, as she did book an appointment. At the appointment, the doctor said that there was nothing wrong with me and sent me and my mum on our way.

I was severely cross-eyed as a baby, and I was barely one year old when I was taken to the optician. They said that I was the youngest person that they had ever given glasses to. When I first wore them, I would pull them straight off my face. My mum had the idea of taking me to a cats' and dogs' home so I would be distracted. When I was at the cats' and dogs' home, I was pulling the glasses off my face for the first 20 minutes, but then I would forget that I was wearing them, as I was looking at the dogs. I then realised that the glasses could make me see better. My mum couldn't get the glasses off me after that. As I was only little, I would regularly break my glasses, and my mum would go to the optician every week to get them fixed. Throughout my life, I have been to three different opticians because they hated fixing my glasses. Each time that my mum walked through the optician's door, all the staff would sigh. Thankfully, I got better at looking after my glasses as I got older.

The thing that highlighted that I had a problem was the walking milestone. The average age that a baby starts to walk is 12 months old. Obviously, some babies start walking earlier or later than this age, but I was very far behind. I was 36 months old before I tried to walk. Before that, I would only roll about.

My mum then knew I had a problem, so she booked another appointment with the doctor and got a referral for a paediatrician and an appointment on her birthday. At the appointment, my mum was told that I did have a problem and it was a problem with my brain. My mum wasn't told what the problem was likely to be but was left to wonder. There was another appointment booked for a month later; this was to diagnose the problem that I had. After that first appointment, she was so upset; she was pushing me home in my pram, thinking it could be anything from brain cancer to genetic conditions that would prove life-limiting. My mum arranged for a physiotherapist to come round and see how my undiagnosed problem was affecting me physically. It was by chance that the physio came round that day, and she was waiting outside my house as me and my crying mum got back from that first appointment. When we got home, the physio asked my mum what was wrong. My mum explained what had just happened at the doctor's and that she didn't know how severe my condition was. The physio reassured my mum by unofficially saying that she would bet her house and pension that I had cerebral palsy. My mum had no clue what that was, and it scared her a little. The physio then explained that I would struggle to walk and use a knife and fork properly, but it wouldn't stop me from being the prime minister if I wanted to one day. Thinking about it, I don't want to be prime minister, but I would hazard a guess I'd do a good job if I was.

From the unofficial diagnosis, I then started to get help. This was mainly through basic physio and stretches that I was encouraged to do and getting supports made for me that I could wear every day. It was at this time I started wearing a day splint and night splint. This would help me keep my foot in the best position for walking. All this help was appreciated, but I still struggled to stay on my feet and walk. The splints were doing me more harm than good as my skin would start to break down because it caused me to sweat. They were uncomfortable which caused me to get a bad night's sleep, so I was tired through the day which caused my leg to be tighter. Wearing the day splint would cause me blisters so I would walk funny to stop the pain. Despite all the troubles with the splints I learnt to walk, but not far. This meant that I would still be carried everywhere.

One month later, we finally went to this appointment, and sure enough, I was diagnosed with moderate left-side cerebral palsy hemiplegia. What did that mean to me at the time? Nothing – I was only three. What did it mean to my mum? It meant that I had something wrong with me and I wasn't 'normal'. My mum couldn't sleep at night thinking how it wasn't fair.

My gran then asked, 'What is the problem?'

This made my mum realise that worrying about it wasn't going to help me, so we just had to get on with life. Also, seeing other kids at appointments who had cerebral palsy much worse than me helped her realise that I wasn't too bad.

On one particular day, I went to my gran's and was wandering around outside. I fell on the corner of the corrugated metal roof that my grandad had off his shed. My mum was working at the local pharmacy at the time, so my gran wheeled me round in a buggy. She then took me to the hospital, where we were told that it was a 'through and through'. There was a hole through both sides of my lip. They sorted that out at the hospital, and I can't remember much more about it. My first war wound was acquired that day thanks to learning how to walk.

This then led on to when I was getting old enough to go to school. My mum just had to find the right one for me. She was interested in a local school so went to have a look around.

My mum told a teacher, 'My son has a disability,' and they replied with 'How disabled is he?'

It was also around this age that I started to realise that I was different from other people and couldn't do the same things as them. I was able to walk but not very well at all. During the visit to the school, the teacher asked to see me walk, but she asked just as all the schoolchildren were coming out for their break. I felt like I had been put on the spot being asked to walk in a straight line in front of all the children. I could have walked if I had wanted to, but I was reluctant as the other kids were there, and I didn't want to fall in front of them. After I didn't walk and so failed to get the teacher's approval, she then said that I was too disabled to go to this school. My mum replied that their school wasn't good enough for me, and we left. She later found out that the school spent the money that they received to help disabled students on flowers for the front of their grounds. It was the right choice not to go to that school.

I was then put into a school that people recommended because it was a good school, not just because they were good with disabled children. My condition was not that bad that I needed to go to a special school, but I would need some extra help at a mainstream school. This school was good at giving me the little extra help that I needed, and that was why they were recommended.

By this point, I stopped wearing the splints because I was given a Lycra sock, arm sleeve and pants. They were much better because they were not painful, and they were also low profile. When I was wearing my day splint it would make me self-conscious because people would stare at me. However, they were an absolute pain to put on every morning.

One of the earliest memories that I have of being at school was trying to thread pasta on a string. I can remember this as it was a hard task for me with my left hand. If I held the string in my left hand, I wouldn't be able to move my fingers out of the way to let the piece of pasta drop down. If I held the string in my right hand, I wouldn't be able to put the thread near the hole through the middle. Another thing that I remember about that is the girl who was sitting next to me was painting a layer of glue on the table. I remember that girl in particular because when I was 14 years old, I found out that she killed herself. Another memory I have from school is Sports Day. Not particularly the day itself but the time in PE that we practised for it. The problem I was having was with the egg-and-spoon race. As my walking was rocky, I would struggle to keep the egg on the spoon. This meant that I wouldn't get very far before dropping it, which meant I was guaranteed to come last. I kept trying my best, but I was coming last every time, and this made me very frustrated. A rage built up inside me, and I lobbed the fake egg across the floor. My teacher wasn't very happy with me. She then asked me to start to behave and try again. I don't know why, but I calmed down and kept trying until PE was over. By the time that sports day came I was given a foot-up which was a sleeve that went around my leg that would clip into a buckle that was attached to my shoe. This would lift the front of my foot up and stop me from falling over. This helped tremendously.

Surprisingly, I became a big brother in July 2008. I wouldn't have thought that my mum would have wanted another child after what her experience was like with me. When my mum went into hospital, I was at my gran's. The next thing I knew, I stopped playing with my Hot Wheels and got into the car to go and see my baby brother Fred. I can remember trying to get comfy in a chair at the hospital so I could hold him. Being a big brother is good, right? My brother had bad colic as a baby, so he was always crying, and when he wasn't, my mum was asleep. I can vividly remember watching *Clifford the Big Red Dog* and the house was quiet for once. He did grow out of the colic (eventually), which helped me so much. People who have cerebral palsy tend to need to get more sleep to function normally. Being able to sleep through the night helped me at school. Being younger – at the age of four to five years old – that did not mean much to me, but as I got older, it definitely meant more. One other positive of having a new brother was getting a platform attached to his buggy; I could stand on the platform, which helped because I still struggled to walk.

From a young age, I was determined to ride a bike without stabilisers, but I kept failing and falling off. We had a small garden, and I would try to learn there, but it was very tight for space, and I was scared of falling on concrete so was reluctant about doing a full send. A full send is what I like to call 'giving your all'. I was wearing gloves and a helmet just in case I did fall off, but the most use my helmet had was not on the bike but when I fell and rolled down the stairs, landing on my head. As I kept trying to ride a bike without stabilisers but was scared of falling off, my confidence kept getting knocked. In the end, I decided just to use my stabilisers.

When I was five years old, my dad left the house. This was because he was not pulling his weight and put unnecessary fears into my mum (like about her driving). To this day, my mum doesn't like to drive, and my dad certainly didn't help with that but made it worse. He would say that she was going to clip the kerb going down narrow roads and would scream, 'We are all going to die!'

I can't really remember what happened, but the last memory I have of living with him was at the house. He was sitting on the couch, leaning on his knees, and the next thing I can remember, he was just gone. Shortly after he left, I started to go and see him on Sundays. From what I can remember, I enjoyed going to my dad when I was young. We would just go out somewhere and spend time together. One of these memories is just going to the cafe nearby.

When my dad left the house, my mum met her ex-boyfriend, Graham, at the pub, and they gradually started seeing each other again. He had seen me previously when he was fixing his race bike outside his mum's house, but our previous brief meeting didn't stop him shaking when we met properly for the first time face to face. This was one night when he was at my house, and I was asleep. I woke up, and we both needed to use the toilet at the same time. I got out of my bed and met him at the top of the stairs, and I remember asking if he was a friend of my mum's. I then went to the toilet and straight back to bed, completely indifferent. I can't say the same about him. Apparently, when he got downstairs, he was shaking and said, 'Well, I met Burt.'

I then started to see Graham more and more, and one thing that he said he will always remember happened on a day where we had been out somewhere. When we got back, I wouldn't walk from the car to the house. It was probably only three car lengths from the car to the front door, but I got halfway and thought I had walked far enough and decided I was not walking any further. I wanted to be carried into the house. I was then left outside. The neighbours were knocking on the door asking my mum whether she knew that I was outside. Fifteen minutes later, I finally got up and went inside by myself. I know that this sounds funny, but it was actually a big moment for me that I walked in the house by myself. This is because at the age of five, I was still used to not walking and being carried everywhere. That is why I stopped halfway and decided that I was not going to walk that little distance. After that happened, I realised that I could walk in the house by myself and started walking more altogether. Another thing that Graham said that he will always remember was him taking me to the park on my bike. Just across the road from where I lived was a park, so I went there often. This particular day, I went out to the park on my bike and was quickly heading towards a narrow gateway. Graham said that he doesn't know how I didn't hit the fence, but I didn't and must have had some balls to do what I did. This is because in the park I was peddling quickly, and I could hear the stabilisers spinning quickly as I went from one side to another. This was when Graham knew that I would be able to ride a bike. He noticed that it was the action of me peddling that was knocking me off balance.

At five years old, I was at the end of the school year and was about to go into Year 1 from Reception, but before the summer holidays, I went and had Botox for the first time. If you do not know what Botox does, I will tell you quickly. It is a chemical that gets injected into muscles. People have this done because it blocks certain chemicals from nerves, which relaxes the muscle. As a little boy, my cerebral palsy was moderate to severe, so Botox was perfect for me. On the day of my operation, I can remember my dad in the driver's seat of the car, taking me and my mum to the hospital, and I was really hungry because I couldn't eat before the operation. I then got my gown on and was wheeled down to the theatre, and my dad came with me. I was then given a toy to play with while I was falling asleep. Next thing I knew, I was waking up with a big table of food. The operation went well – a little too well, in fact. The Botox made my leg useless. This was not the doctor's fault but a possible side effect of having Botox. This is because Botox affects people differently, just like alcohol; some people need a lot, and some need a little to feel the effect. I only needed a little. To rectify the problem, I was then in serial casting until I gained the use of my leg back. This was not the best news, as I would be in a cast for most of the school holidays.

Serial casting involves setting limbs in an ideal position so that the body will adapt, and it helps improve movement after weeks of having the casts on. When the first cast was put on, it was to stay on for a couple weeks, and then I would have another one put on after that. I liked going on the train to get a new cast because it was a day out for me, and I didn't have to go to school. I can remember before school broke up, I was walking round the playground wearing a sock over my cast and wearing a sandal. It was pretty cold, and having a heavy cast on my leg meant it wasn't easy to walk, but on the whole, I wasn't bothered. My serial casting was to last a total of six weeks, and I got my last cast off towards the end of the summer holidays.

During the summer holidays, I went to the childminder's a few times a week, as my mum was at work and there was no one else to look after me. Before going into Year 1, I broke my leg at the childminder's. I broke my leg just 10 days after the last round of serial casting. It happened when I was on the trampoline with a kid that was bigger and heavier than me. I was in the middle of sitting down with my legs crossed as the other kid landed after doing a high jump. CRACK. Just like that, my good leg was broken.

I can't remember how I got into the house, but I managed it. I was just sitting on the couch while the childminder told my mum what had happened and that she needed to come and collect me. While I was waiting to be picked up, I can remember the deep throbbing pain that came in waves. It got even worse when I put a bag of cold peas on my leg. My mum phoned my gran to pick me up to go to hospital. My gran drove me there, as my mum was afraid of driving to hospital. My gran didn't like driving either, but she could get to the hospital. Between remembering the throbbing pain at the childminder's and getting to A&E, the only memory that I have was the pain getting worse in the car as we sped up, slowed down or went round corners.

When we got to hospital, I managed to walk from the car park to the waiting room on both legs with a helping hand from my mum.

When I was seen by a doctor, he did not think that I'd broken my leg because I didn't look like I was in enough pain. He wasn't even going to do an X-ray because he didn't think I needed one. However, my mum persuaded him to send me for one. The results showed that I had a fracture below the knee. The nurses put bandages round my leg for compression; this was to stop the swelling and bruising, which was to last for the first two days. It was only on the way out that the doctor told my mum that if it wasn't for me having cerebral palsy and recently being out of serial casting, he would have sent us on our way. He said that he had seen full-grown adults with the same break as I had bawling their eyes out because it hurt that much. He then proceeded to ask if I wanted extra medication, but I said, 'I think I am fine for now, but it still hurts a bit.'

I was complaining more about being hungry as I hadn't eaten anything but my breakfast all day. My mum felt really sorry for me because I had only been out of a cast for 10 days and was now back in one for another eight weeks, so on the way home, she stopped off at the takeaway and got me a chicken burger. I then said that it was the best burger that I had ever eaten and didn't seem bothered about my leg because I couldn't have changed what had happened. I just accepted wearing yet another cast.

Graham then came round to separate the bunk beds that me and my brother shared because I usually slept on the top bunk and with my cast, I couldn't get in the bottom because the ladders were in the way.

After waiting a few days for the swelling to go down, we went to the children's hospital, where they were able to fit a cast. This really hurt, as they had to bend my leg into a certain position so that it would heal right. They took their time doing this, as it was very important it was done correctly. The cast that I had put on ended up being from my hip all the way down to the foot. This caused the cast to be a heavy lump that I had to carry round with me. I was then in a wheelchair for the next eight weeks.

With my right leg being in a cast the next eight weeks, I started to use my left leg for everyday tasks. One of the challenges was standing on my left leg while brushing my teeth at the sink. Doing activities like these on my left leg only built up its strength.

School then started a week after I broke my leg. My gran volunteered to come into school and take care of me. She quit her job to do this. If she hadn't, then I would have had to stay at home for seven weeks, as my mum was currently a single mother. She also had to look after my brother, who was still only 18 months old. I couldn't afford to not be in school, as I had the same numeracy and literacy skills as a kid in nursery. This was because I spent my time learning how to walk instead of learning the alphabet and basic reading.

My gran then started coming into school with me to help as my assistant. She would push me to class, to the dinner hall and to the computer room. I even had my own toilets at the front of school, next to the reception. All the kids in my class were understanding and wanted to know what had happened. In the playground, my friends would ask if they could push me in my wheelchair. My gran used to let them help her but would always have her hands on the handles. One memory that I can remember was when someone coloured in a drawing of a parrot and stuck it onto my wheelchair.

One day, my gran took me to the dinner hall, and a new policy was in place that you needed to use your knife and fork. The school put my gran to work at dinner, cleaning tables, etc. As I struggled to use my left hand, I would not use my knife in my left hand, and a dinner lady was saying that I needed to use both hands and was not being very nice to me. My gran was in earshot of the conversation and told the head teacher what happened and how the staff were not disability friendly. My gran did not get a response back from the school after this, but I never had an incident like that happen again.

Considering what had happened, all was going well until I accidentally stood in dog poo, and it went all over the cast. I couldn't keep this cast on and had to get it changed. My mum took me to the children's hospital, and it was so busy that we ended up going to A&E instead, and they changed the cast there. I can remember the nurses taking the cast off and putting a new one on. As soon as the cast stopped supporting my leg, it started aching and was uncomfortable, but my leg was better a few hours later.

A few days later, I complained to my mum that my leg was sore. I then went and visited my dad, and he took me and my brother to go and see my nan. While I was there, my leg was sore and started to itch, so I tried to scratch the itch using a knitting needle. This made the sensation worse. I then told my mum when I got home, and she asked if I wanted to get another cast put on, but it was going to be taken off in five days anyway. I could not be bothered with getting another one put on, so I dealt with the discomfort for the time remaining. When I got the cast off, there was a cut in the side of my leg where a little bit of the cast had splintered off and dug in. The scar was so big from the cast that it is still visible now, over 10 years later.

Not using my right leg for eight weeks meant that I suffered from muscle wastage. However, it only took two days to recover from that. After I gained strength back in my right leg, my mum said that was the best that I had ever walked in my life. The extra strength and mobility that I gained from the serial casting and as a result of breaking my leg was the perfect recipe for my walking to get better. As my walking had got a lot better since I broke my leg I stopped wearing splints and the different supports to help me. I have never worn them since that day. I still kept getting them from the hospital every time I went because the doctors would push for me to wear them. It was easier to take them home instead of arguing your reason not to have them. Why wear the splints if you don't need them?

Six to eight years old

I started to see Graham at the house a lot more and was therefore spending a lot of time with him – we would play games on the Nintendo Wii and such like. It was at this point that I went up to my mum and asked if I could call him Dad. She didn't expect me to ask that question but said of course I could if I wanted to. I then went up to him and asked if I could call him Dad, and he said I could call him whatever I wanted. It was at this point that he became my 'dad'. I've thought about the best way to make the book easier to read, so I am still going to call Graham by his name to make it easier to follow.

Year 1 was a year I spent trying to catch up with all the other children in my class. In terms of academic ability. Although I spent the whole year trying my hardest, I was still three years behind everyone else and academically was doing the same work as those in nursery.

In Year 2, I had a bad experience with my teacher while doing PE. I joined in with the PE lessons at primary school, but one day, I was made to do something that I was not able to do. In PE, we were walking across the benches that were in the school hall while they were turned upside down. At the bottom of these benches was a narrow support beam that was just big enough to get your foot on. The first thing that I remember is being in the line waiting for my turn to walk across this upturned bench. I was nervous when I got to the front of the line, but I got up onto the bench with my right foot first. I then placed my left in front of the other successfully, which was a struggle, as I do not have full control of my left leg. The next step was to move my right foot in front of my left foot. Wobbling on my left foot and with my arms out by my sides, I was able to stay on the beam. After I did it with both feet, I felt confident, but that was to crumble when I had to move my left foot next. I didn't place it on the narrow beam perfectly straight, and this caused me to lose my balance. To counteract the loss of balance, I quickly tried to progress forward, but that came to no avail when I fell off the bench. I then had to catch myself by moving my right foot, and then my feet were crossed with my left foot still on the bench and my right foot on the floor.

I had a quick look behind me to see if the people from my class had seen what had happened, and they had, but they didn't think anything of what I had done. I then proceeded to try and jump back on the beam with my right leg. After trying and making myself look like a fool, I finally got back on the beam only to fall off again because I couldn't keep my balance. My teacher then got involved, telling me that I needed to hurry up to let the other kids have a go. With me making a fool of myself and holding up the line as I was making little progress, a minute passed – if the other kids weren't bothered about me, they were going to be soon. My teacher started losing her patience at this point, so I just got off the beam and began to sulk at the back of the line. I wasn't going to get back on the beam again.

My teacher then started to have a go at me for quitting and not completing the task. She was not just my PE teacher; she was my class teacher and should have known my capabilities. So when I said that I couldn't do it and that I wasn't going to try it again and again, she should have left me alone, but she didn't. This was the first time that I can remember where I was doing an activity like this, an activity that would test my balance. When in the line, I was unsure whether I was going to be able to do it or not in the first place. I did give it a go and failed, but I didn't give up straight away either. I kept trying before I knew what I was trying to do was too hard for me. Although I couldn't do the beam, I should have had the chance to try a similar but easier activity.

I went back home and told my parents what had happened that day, and they were furious. Graham is very short and blunt, and I remember him saying to me, 'I would like to see her fat ass do what she asked you to do!' I was put off doing PE because I didn't want a situation like that to happen again. There was then a meeting with the head teacher, my parents and my teacher. I can't fully remember as it was so long ago, but I think she had a warning for what she had done and didn't turn up to school for weeks. I thought that she had left. It couldn't have been that, though, because I didn't get a new teacher. We had a substitute teacher for what seemed to me a couple of weeks, and sure enough, she was my teacher again for the rest of the year. After this incident, I was treated so much better than before, and my teacher was so, so careful about what she said to my parents. I think that she was a little scared of them, so whatever happened at that meeting must have been severe for her.

The only good that came out of Year 2 was that I made a massive jump academically and went from being three years behind to only two years behind everyone else. This meant that I was making double the progress that people in my class were making. This was because my walking had significantly improved, and I could focus on my schoolwork instead. During my time at primary school, I worked hard to reduce how far behind I was and made progress every year.

Throughout my childhood, I used to go fishing with my gran multiple times a year. At a very young age, my gran wouldn't let me set the rod up – firstly because it was dangerous but secondly because I didn't know what I was doing. While we were fishing, my gran would let me try to hook a maggot to the hook on the end of the line. She would then take over, as I would try to do it but wasn't able to. She said it was because I couldn't hold the hook in my left hand without losing my grip. If I didn't lose my grip, my left hand would shake, which made putting bait on the end of the line hard with my right hand. Trying to hook a maggot onto a moving target is harder than it looks. Eventually, after my hand started to shake, it would then get fatigued and drop the hook anyway. To let you know how much use I had in my left hand in other areas of my life this was about it. I could hold down a piece of toast in my left hand to cut it with my right hand while chasing it round the worktops. As the hook was so much smaller, I found that my hand would shake uncontrollably.

Now that I am older, I still like to go fishing from time to time, and I can bait up my line. I now set up my fishing rod by myself, and that is tough because there are new challenges. The first one is threading the line through the eyelets on the rod. It isn't just me that struggles with this, but I struggle more than the average person would. As I've got older, I've found little hacks that make certain tasks easier, I can use them to help me thread my rod. The unique ways I do certain things like threading a rod work for me because of how my cerebral palsy affects me personally. For this reason, the solutions that I use to get round problems will not work for everyone, and you need to find your own. The next challenge is actually tying the hook onto the line. This is where you need to wrap the line around itself multiple times. I can just about manage it. It takes me a lot longer than other people, but I persevere.

It isn't all bad news, though. As you can imagine, fishing on your own can be pretty boring. I went fishing with my gran last year when the Covid restrictions were starting to lift, but some were still enforced. At the pond where we fish, the owners were only letting one person on a peg at a time, but with my disability, I could say that my gran was helping me by getting my rod ready. I could have done that by myself, but it is no lie that my gran was giving me a useful helping hand. This meant that I could spend a day fishing with someone to talk to.

When I was seven years old, I was on a mission to try and learn how to tie shoelaces. My mum tried showing me how to tie them for hours. Graham noticed that I was getting confused because my mum was opposite me, and that meant that what my mum was doing looked backwards to me. When Graham pointed that out, that confused my mum because she has dyslexia and couldn't wrap her head around what Graham was saying. He then tied the laces from my perspective on my side and showed me how to do it. After countless hours trying, I finally started to get the idea of how to do it and was able to do the right movements involved. The problem that I faced was that I could not wrap the lace around the other lace that was looped tight, so when I did the knot and pulled both loops, the ends would fall out. To combat this, Graham gave me his work boots to practise on, as the laces were very long and the knot would tighten up without the ends falling out. I was able to tie the laces on the work boots and now had to do the knots on my own shoes. This was hard, as the laces were not as long as those on the work boots. This caused me to struggle for the next two years while I practised tying laces that would not come undone.

Every morning, I would tie my own shoes before I went to school. The short walk from the car to the classroom would cause the laces to come undone numerous times. My mum would offer to tie them for me, but I would tell her, 'I am not a baby, and I can do them myself.'

She would then watch me struggle for 10 minutes while I tied my shoes again. This would cause me to get to class late. Over this two-year period, I learnt to tie them myself properly, but then I would grow, and my hand would get worse. I would then have to start from scratch again and relearn how to tie my shoelaces. My mum had to look after my brother and get him ready in the morning and therefore would leave me to practise tying my laces myself instead of helping me. If Fred wasn't there, she would just have to watch me struggle. When I was finally able to tie my own shoelaces, this gave me independence. With a sense of independence, I would not need a grown-up to do them for me but could look after myself.

When I was diagnosed with left-side cerebral palsy, the doctor told me and my mum that I would most likely never be able to ride a bike. Now that I am 17 years old, motorbikes are a big part of my life. I think that this was inevitable, as I come from a family full of bikers. I tried to learn how to ride a bike multiple times when I was younger with no success, which caused me to throw the towel in. At this point in my life, I was no longer bothered to ride a bike. I accepted that I could not do it. That was until my younger brother Fred learnt before I did – he was only four years old. For one reason or another, this lit a raging fire within me that made me want to learn how to ride. I wasn't going to let my younger brother ride a bike while I couldn't do it.

One morning, I got dropped off at my gran's, and she found an old bike that was my uncle's, which was given to him when he was four or five years old. My grandad checked it over, and it was ready for me. This bike was very small for me, but I had a go. There was a small hill going up to my gran's drive. I got to the brow of the hill and pushed myself off. As I started moving, I placed my feet on the pedals and kept my balance. On the next run, I started to push the pedals lightly. Every run that I did, I started pushing the pedals gradually harder. This worked, as the momentum of going down the hill counteracted the side force of peddling. After I had spent the whole morning practising, my mum came back to pick me up, and she was amazed at what she saw. She had a mix of emotions but was happy for me overall: she was excited that I was finally able to ride a push bike, but she was also angry at my gran, as she wanted me to feel ready to face this task again when the cerebral palsy was not affecting me as badly. There was a greater risk of falling and feeling disheartened when my arm and leg were not the best and I was struggling to use them. With my ability to travel some distance at the bottom of the hill from my own pedal power, my family saw so much potential and brought the tiny bike back to the house. My mum was still not happy that my gran had let me on a bike because it might have turned out differently.

I still struggled riding the bike. This was partly because of the size of the bike; however, the coordination of my legs was the main factor. I spent hours riding that bike on the street. The older kids on the street were making fun of me, saying that I couldn't ride a bike properly and was riding a bike meant for a baby. Those comments did not matter to me, as I was hyper-focused on riding. I dedicated myself so much that I developed a blister that covered over half of my left hand. When that burst, I was still riding with the handlebars rubbing against the live skin, as I wanted to gain more confidence. After my parents saw how many hours I was putting in, they got me a bike as a celebration/reward. I remember being so happy having a bike that looked like the other kids' on the street.

Now I could ride a push bike, Graham wanted to see if I could ride a motorbike. This was when he bought a mini-moto and modified it so that I would fit on it (again, I was a little big for it). The next holiday we went on was to a Prestatyn caravan park. We put the mini-moto in the boot of the car and took it along with us. Throughout the week, we went on the beach with the bike, and this was where my first successful motorbike ride happened. When I got on the beach, I got all geared up and had to get my mum to help me put my gloves on, as I couldn't do it myself.

At first, I sat at the front of the bike with Graham on the back as an instructor. He was showing me how to use and control the throttle correctly. I was actually riding a motorbike! After building up confidence and trust with him on the back for a bit, I rode the bike by myself. I ended up doing so many laps going up and down the beach. With my family extremely proud of me, Graham started recording my laps and turned my riding into a video. This was how I started riding motorbikes. Yeah, I really did do what the doctors said was near impossible by not only riding a push bike but riding a motorbike as well. That just makes the doctors look silly, doesn't it? Saying that, I still did need help from my mum putting my gloves on.

My dad found a girlfriend, and I met her when I went to see him one Sunday. She had her own flat and her own children as well. I found it weird that my dad was getting himself a girlfriend. It wasn't just one extra person that I would be seeing on Sundays, but her children, too. I didn't mind her children – in fact, I got on well with them – but what I didn't like was them taking my dad's attention. Before he met his girlfriend, he used to take me and my brother for days out, and we would be busy; after he met his girlfriend, we started to stay at home instead of going out somewhere.

Eight to ten years old

As I went into Year 3, I could do extra music lessons, and I decided to learn the drums. Having drumming lessons was a good idea for me because you have to synchronise both arms and legs to make a good beat. Once a week, I had a drumming lesson with other people at school. I didn't take to the drums straight away, but I also didn't have a hard time starting to learn how to use them either – I was in the middle of the road, I guess. The first thing that I was taught was the standard four beats and how to spice it up a little. This took many weeks to do because the only practice that I had was the one hour a week that was shared with other students. After a while, it was noticed by my parents that my left arm was getting stronger, which was partly why I joined in the first place.

As well as the drumming that I was doing, I also had to do compulsory music lessons, and the two choices were between the cello and the violin. There was a minuscule chance that I would be able to play the violin, so I opted for the cello. I was no good at this either, but I had to do it. This was because you use the bow in the right hand, and I was unable to use my left hand to make the right notes. I did try to swap my hands, but I couldn't even make a sound on the instrument. I tried in the lessons that I had but couldn't wait to stop doing them, as I found playing near impossible. The songs that I managed to half-play sounded terrible.

Even though I struggled to play the cello, I was making considerable progress playing the drums.

At eight years old, I needed something to do outside of school, so I joined the local football team. It was my mum's idea for me to join a team to keep myself physically active, and I did not mind it either because I could see my friends from school. At the start of my football journey, I was nowhere near as good as the other players; I was tripping over nearly 10 times a match. We trained twice a week and then played matches on the weekends. Obviously, it was important that I got better, but the team had players of mixed ability. There was one player on my team who was that tall he was like a newborn giraffe still learning how to use his legs. Then there was another player, a year younger than the rest of us, who was running circles round everyone and scoring all the goals. Then there was me trying to find my place on the pitch. In my opinion, this is what made the team good. Players who struggled and players who were naturally gifted were there because they liked football.

My position on the team was right-back. I was starting to get so good my team was calling me 'the wall' because I would not let the other team past. I was always able to set a play up from the back when I had the ball. I wear glasses, and this was a problem for the team; I got the ball kicked at my face on three different occasions. Each time, this broke my glasses and cut my face up, but that did not stop me playing the rest of the matches. After that happened so many times, my coach said that I needed to get a pair of sports glasses so they wouldn't break again. I did not like the look of sports glasses and did not want to wear them playing football, so I wrote a letter to my coach saying that I would quit the team if I had to wear them. I continued playing for the team with my own glasses.

Another injury that I got playing football was when my own teammate kicked my ankle. The ball was near our net. We both went to clear the ball, but I got to it first, which led to him kicking my ankle. As I limped off the pitch, my parents said that I could swear if it made me feel better. In front of all the other parents, I said, 'Fucking hell, that hurts!' or something along those lines, but my mum said that I had strung the best swear words together, and I wasn't even that old. I was only nine or ten at the time, but the worst part of that was that it was friendly fire, so I didn't even get a free kick. It was a lot more embarrassing to be on my mum's end of things with pretty much everybody hearing what I'd said about my ankle.

We trained at a field near my primary school and could be travelling up to 20 miles to play a match. The team got used to how all the players played, the chemistry of the team grew, and the team got better and started winning more matches. Playing football helped keep me active, and my physio could see the benefits.

What was so good about the team that I joined was that it was friendly; we were not really competitive – just a group of kids from school who wanted to have fun. The parents were not overly involved in the kids' football either. I liked the team and wanted to join in with what they were doing, which led to what happened with my dad.

Since my dad left the house, I was seeing him on most Sundays, and there weren't many problems. But there was a problem on Remembrance Sunday, and here is why: I wanted to do the Remembrance walk with my football team. This wouldn't have stopped him seeing me that day if he had taken me to do it, but he didn't want to. However, he especially wanted to see me that day because it was my birthday. My birthday lands on Remembrance Sunday one year out of seven, and it was that year when it happened. My dad didn't think about what I would have wanted and only thought of himself. I remember going to see him that Sunday, but I didn't know why I remembered that Sunday in particular. To get to my dad's house, I had to go past the ceremony in the car, which teased me in a way. After a little while at his house, we then went to my nan's so I could open my birthday present while my dad could speak to his mum. I then went back to his house and watched a film until I went home. I remember that day being a bit of a waste, as it was my birthday and all I did in essence was watch a film and open my present from my nan when I wanted to do the walk of respect.

When I was nine, my mum had my half-brother with Graham, and he is called Joe. He was called Joe because Graham likes motorbikes; Joe was named after Joey Dunlop, a motorcycle racer whose race number was three – Joe is the third child. As a present for me being an even bigger brother now and my little brother becoming a big brother, we were given chains. I remember going into school wearing this chain, and they were not happy, as it wasn't part of the uniform. So, from then on, I couldn't wear it. It was too hard for me to take it off and put it back on again by myself with my bad hand. I can't remember what happened to that chain, but I was annoyed a couple of years later when I thought of it but didn't know where it was.

Joe was active even before he turned one. He learnt how to walk at eight months old, escaped the house at one year old and wasn't even three when he learnt how to ride a bike. To escape the house, he had to climb over a baby gate at the top of the stairs and then get down the stairs to another baby gate at the bottom. He used this baby gate to get the keys that were on a hook on the wall and then unlocked the door and was halfway down the street with the dog before we realised he had escaped.

It was around the time Joe was born when I started swimming in school. Every Monday after I ate my lunch, me and my class would get onto the minibus and go to the local baths, where we would learn how to swim. We would have our lesson, get dressed and be back at school for home time.

I can only remember snippets of my time in the water. I think the first thing that we all did was get in the pool and put our faces under the water. My next snippet is swimming the length of the small pool with armbands. We did this for a few weeks. Then, I was given armbands that aided me less, as did everyone else. More time passed, and we weren't able to use armbands at all. I really started to struggle and was near drowning at that point, when I was told to swim the width of the small pool. I was JUST able to do that and was given my armbands back, which I was thankful for, but at the same time pissed off because I was not progressing at the same rate as everyone else. By this time, everyone else was going into the big pool.

My next snippet is trying to swim the length of the small pool with no armbands. I was managing well until I got about halfway across. All of a sudden, my arms and legs decided to give up on me. It was only by sheer determination that I was able to keep myself moving. The last half of the journey felt like it took 10 minutes, as I kept having to hold my breath while my head was bobbing in and out of the water because I was busy thinking about jump-starting my arms and legs. By some miracle, I got to the other side.

Next Monday, I was told to go in the big pool, and I metaphorically shit myself. I was in that pool until my school lessons ended. I can't actually tell you what I did in there up until then, except life preservation. One thing that I can tell you for certain is I was not doing lengths of the pool.

After I finished the swimming with school, I was still not able to swim properly, so my mum got me 10 extra lessons. The swimming baths made an error giving my mum a price. They quoted me 'one-on-one' lessons for the price of group lessons. I can't remember much about these lessons except feeling a little pressured because someone was watching my every move for an hour. With that happening, however, I did make progress. By the time that the extra lessons were finished, I was sort of able to swim. By no means was I a strong or confident swimmer. After swimming with school and the extra lessons, I have gone in the pool every time that I have gone away on holiday and got better at doing it. I've not swum in years, but I am confident enough in my ability that if I needed to swim to save my life, I could.

When I was nine, Graham got me a PW50 motorbike. This was bigger and faster than the mini-moto. I rode this bike on the fields at the local park. It was early into the year, so the ground was still damp. Graham thought that I was skilled enough to learn to slide the bike going around the corner. The first day went great; I got used to the new bike and started to slide the rear end going round corners. The next session stands out in my memory. I was riding the PW50 and my friends were walking across the park, so I wanted to show them how good I was. I slid round the corner, but a stick went through my wheel, and I fell off. Graham thought I fell off being too cocky.

He took me to the rough ground by the canal, but I did not like riding on it, as I thought it was too bumpy. Fred hadn't ridden the PW50 before, but he decided that day he wanted a go. He got on the bike and started moving. As this was his first go on the PW50, he wasn't used to the faster speeds and ended up riding into a ditch of brambles.

I had a problem one Christmas Day with my dad where it went all pear-shaped. It was my dad's turn to have me and my brother for Christmas. I didn't really want to go in the first place. I wanted to stay at my house and have Christmas there. My mum tried telling my dad that I didn't want to go round that day but that he could see me and my brother on Boxing Day. My dad was adamant that I should come round, as it was his time to see me – the same reaction he'd had on Remembrance Sunday. I wasn't looking forward to going, so my mum gave me a phone to use in case I wanted to come home. I went and it wasn't that bad, but it did feel wrong being there with my stepsiblings. As my dad was making Christmas dinner, I just thought that it wasn't right not being at my house, so I went to the toilet and phoned my mum to come and pick me up. A little while later, my mum came to pick me and my brother up and knocked on the door. After there was some confusion as to why they were there, I finally got to the car and sat in the car for a while before my mum and Graham got back and took me and my brother home. I still didn't feel right at my house straight away. I think I needed to calm down and try not to feel guilty. As the day went on, I slowly forgot about it.

After Christmas, I received Botox for the second time, as I started to have another growth spurt and was struggling to walk again. Let me explain why my walking got worse while I was growing. When 'normal' children grow they become a little clumsy. One reason for this is that bones grow quicker than muscles making the muscles tighter than normal. As my muscles are naturally tight and spastic it just exaggerated the problem, and I was walking with a major limp.

It all started with a routine visit to the children's hospital, and we talked about different ideas that might work. The doctor said that another patient had cancelled their operation on late notice and that I could have Botox if I wanted. The operation was the following day. I didn't want it, but my mum decided that it was best for me to have it done. I started begging my mum in the doctor's office not to have it. On the way home, I was shouting at my mum and asking why she had agreed to it. She said it was her decision, which I didn't think was fair, but she said she couldn't change it now as the operation was tomorrow. I then shut up. As I couldn't eat for a day before the operation, I had a takeaway that night. The one thing that I was promised I would get for having Botox again was Xbox Live Gold for the Xbox that I got for Christmas – this was so I could play with my friends online.

The next day, we got up early. When I arrived at the hospital, I just accepted what was happening. The first time I had Botox, the doctors learnt that I was overly sensitive to it, so this time, I did not have as much, and it worked as it should. After I came back from the theatre, I woke up and my leg was stinging where they had put the injections. While I was waiting for my doctor to see me, I was in a ward with many other kids who had been in there for weeks. I remember one of them being in there for six weeks (because I think he had cancer), but it didn't stop him from being happy to speak to me. Looking back, it was stupid how I acted after I got out of hospital just because I'd had Botox. On the way home, I sat in the front of the car, and my mum sat in the back. I wasn't speaking to her because I was still angry with her, but I was speaking to Graham because he was telling my mum that maybe it was best I didn't get the Botox done the day before. he was also my friend because he got me a Mars bar and a bottle of vanilla Coke. It took days for me to speak to my mum again.

After Christmas Day, I didn't see my dad for weeks – it wasn't until court finished (over my dad's access) and it was decided that I could go and see him again at a visitation centre. I found this very weird, as I would get dropped off by Graham to go see my dad for a little bit.

The visitation centre was an old church, and it wasn't the closest to our house. To me, it felt like I spent just as much time in the car travelling to go and see him as I actually spent with him. I went there a few times and played Connect 4 and then left. As weird as I found it going to a church to see my dad, I liked that it was just me and my dad instead of everyone else. After so many weeks, I could then go round to my dad's house again. All was going well, but it was only going to last for so long, wasn't it? Little did I know at that point in time that he didn't learn from past experiences.

Ten to twelve years old

Fred saw me drumming while he went to pick me up with my mum and wanted to have a go as well. He was only five or six but was begging to have a go. This was when we got a battered drum kit so I could practise at home and my teacher could give my little brother lessons. Fred wasn't old enough to have them at school. Me and my brother shared a room at this point, and the drum kit was in our room. With the lessons at home, my brother took to it like a fish in water and came along quick at a young age.

It was around this time that I wanted to use the last name Rickman and asked whether it could be changed. Rickman is Graham's surname, and I saw him so much as my dad even at that age that I wanted to change my name from Huziej to Rickman. My mum said that my dad would need to sign the name change deed, but she thought that he wouldn't want to sign it. She then came up with the idea that I should start writing my name as Rickman on all my books at school and such. This was in an effort to see if that would work somehow in the future.

By this time, my dad and his girlfriend were married. I honestly can't remember much about the wedding, but what I can remember I can't put into words. I thought my family at my house was separate from the family that my dad was in. I would go to visit my dad, but I would also see my stepsiblings at the same time. Even though I saw my stepsiblings every Sunday, I couldn't see them as part of my family. This doesn't mean that I didn't like them. I actually welcomed the fact that the two families were separated, as I would see them only when I met my dad. This changed one Sunday when my dad asked how I had found the primary school that I was currently going to at that point in time. The reason was because my stepmum didn't have a car and had to walk my stepbrother to his school, which was far away, every day.

A few weeks later, I found out my stepbrother was going to the same school as me. I didn't mind this, but the problem was my stepmum. She would come up to me in the playground and insist that I gave her a hug. It felt forced, and I didn't like what was happening, so one week when my mum was waking me up for school, I said that I was ill so I didn't have to go into the playground. My mum then arranged that I would go to my class through the reception at the front of the school so my stepmum wouldn't ask for a hug. My mum has told me that my dad would go into the school complaining that I shouldn't be allowed to go through reception to avoid seeing my stepmum. My school then wondered why me and my brother walking through reception to get into school was a problem for my dad and my stepmum. If anything, that encounter confirmed why I wanted to walk through the front of the school in the first place.

One break time, a girl came up to me and asked why I didn't like my stepbrother, so I told her why – I was just being honest. I said that he had only come to this school to stalk me. As soon as I said that, I knew I shouldn't have and regretted it as soon as she walked away. The girl in my class then told my stepbrother what I had said, but I didn't know that she had done that. Obviously, I was told why he had moved to the same school as me – which is more than a valid reason – but to me, it felt like they just wanted to follow me because my stepmum was insisting that I hugged her in the playground.

The next Sunday, I went to my dad's house. My mum had a feeling that something was going to happen that day so gave my brother, who was six years old, a phone. In the car on the way there, my dad didn't say a word. I knew something was wrong then; I started connecting the dots. I had a feeling that he had found out what I said at school and was angry at that. I went through the front door and was brought into the living room, where my stepmum and dad questioned why I had said what I said, so what did I do? I told them exactly what I said to the girl.

I said, 'I feel like you moved my stepbrother to my school so you could stalk me.'

They didn't like what I had just said and told me to apologise, but believing in what I said, I was unable to apologise. I was then made to stand in the corner of the room until I apologised. My brother was kept occupied on his phone on my dad's knee so that he didn't really notice what was happening. I thought that I wouldn't be made to stand for long, but I was wrong. I stood for so long that my legs started to ache, and I was swapping which leg took most of my weight so the other could have a rest. My left leg was struggling. I asked if I could go to the toilet, not that I needed to use it but because I wanted to rest my legs. I didn't stay in the bathroom for too long, as I thought it would look suspicious. I came back downstairs, and both parents went into the kitchen quickly. I tried to get my brother's attention, but he was too busy with a game. I was trying to get him to give me the phone so I could phone home. My dad and stepmum then came back in, and I thought it was ridiculous what was happening and thought about walking out the house to go home. My house was a mile and a half away. I was 10 years old, but the only thing that stopped me was my little brother. He was six at the time, and I didn't know whether he would come with me and be able to make it home or whether he would just stay at my dad's house. Eventually, my dad sat me down and asked if I wanted to come anymore, and I didn't know what to say. I said no, and my brother revealed that we had a phone just in case we wanted to use it. My dad then said a few words and brought us home. That was the last time, until recently, that I saw him. Otherwise, I've seen him in the shops and in his car but haven't spoken to him in seven years.

After all that happened at my dad's that day, it was clearly going to be unpleasant attending the same school as my stepbrother, so I switched schools. My mum was thinking about me going to another school anyway, but after what happened with my dad, I definitely wanted to move school. The other reason that I might have moved school anyway was to get into a good high school. The primary school that I was already at meant that it was most likely I'd end up going into a high school that had been put into special measures by the government. The primary school that I ended up moving to was a feeder school to a top-rated high school, so I was guaranteed a place there.

I had a look round the new school, and it seemed alright, but the main thought that I had was how small it was compared to my previous school. I couldn't find a reason why I didn't like the school so went there for the last three weeks of Year 5. Fred stayed at the other school because they had no places for him. Without Graham, it would have been impossible to go to this new school because my mum couldn't be in two places at once, and she couldn't drop me off at one school and drop my brother off at another. So, for the last few weeks of the school year, I went to school on the back of Graham's motorbike. It was at this point my love for bikes grew, as we would take the long way to school so we were able to spend more time on the bike doing faster speeds.

It was around this point that I quit the football team. It went downhill for me when the trainer left. The new coach was not kind, and some of the players left to go to other teams. I left during one training session when we were doing laps of the pitch. If someone stopped, the new coach – who was apparently an ex-professional – threatened to kick the ball in their face. I did not like his attitude, so I just walked off and left training mid-session.

The next time that the physio came round, I told her that I had stopped playing football. She told me about a team called CP United and recommended that I have a look at it. My mum phoned up and asked if I could come down, and they were happy for me to. The first thing that I noticed when I got there was the varying degrees of cerebral palsy that people had. The first thing that my mum noticed (which shocked her) was how other parents were caring for their kids excessively, running onto the pitch to give their kid a drink. There was a massive contrast between my old team and the new team that I joined in both player ability and the team atmosphere. There were kids who were using Zimmer frames and kids who were better than me, so there was a wide range of abilities.

What I came to find was that there was not exactly a team for my age; I was 11 at the time. This meant that I was in between the foundation team and the team with the older players in there. I was able to play with the kids who were older than me; in fact, I went on a day out to play at the Nottingham 2015 CPISRA World Games. I was not playing for England, but all the other teams would come and watch England – I remember watching England vs Japan. When England were not playing, our U15s team would play friendlies against other teams, and I was good and got involved. The day started early and ended late, so it was a busy day, but before I left, I got a shirt signed by some of the England players, and I still have that today. On the way home, we were on a brand-new coach, and it had a toilet at the back. I got a phone call off my mum saying that Graham was coming to pick me up on his motorbike, so on the way back, I was getting changed in the toilet.

I started boxing when my football was not as good because of the coach changing. I started boxing not because I was specifically interested but because there was a gym local to us and I hadn't tried it before. The boxing gym had a weekly session called 'The Little Rockys'.

I remember walking into the gym for the first time. The gym was upstairs, and as I got closer to the top of the stairs, there was a smell of sweat that got worse. When I opened the door, everybody was working hard – no wonder there was a bad smell! I was a little older than the other children there, but the next class for me was for teenagers/adults who were a lot older than me and who were training for their amateur fights. My little brother also joined me at these sessions.

The first session that I attended was footwork, stance and guard. I had to put gloves on to do this, and they also smelt vile. This was the first time that I did any fight-based training, and it didn't feel natural to me. Footwork I managed to get my head around quite quickly I thought, and I was able to move in all directions fluidly. Stance was a little harder: trying to keep on my toes and distribute my weight was tough while thinking about combinations and guard. Guard was not physically hard for me, but my left hand would drop from my cheek if I was not conscious about what it was doing. At the end of that session, I took my gloves off and was nearly sick at the smell of my hands. You didn't need to have a shower to get clean after but to make your hands smell better.

Learning to throw punches is what I can remember most about The Little Rockys, as the difference in power between my two arms was what I found to be the most frustrating. In boxing, your weaker side will be used as the leading hand, which is the jab. That means that the other side is used as the backhand or power hand. This was not helping the discrepancy in power that I felt purely because of the nature of the style that boxing uses. I understood that in boxing there was this difference, but for me with my weak side, I didn't know how big of a gap the difference should be. This wound me up because I didn't know if I was just the same as everyone else. It would be really hard to measure the punching force of my weaker left arm compared to someone else's left arm, to see how far from the average I was.

The training sessions were warm-up, technical work, cardio/bag work, and sometimes you could also punch the coach at the end of the session. My coach told my mum that I had one hell of a punch on my right side, and it was as strong as some adults. Even at a young age, I was happy to hear that, but I still knew that I could only tickle my opponent with my left hand, which was no good. Effectively from then on in boxing, I knew my right hand was the only weapon that would deal proper damage.

At this point, my mum was big into her fitness, got good at running, wanted to join the local gym and thought it was a good idea if I could join, too, even though I was young. We spoke to the person at the gym about what I was looking for, but I was two years too young, so we lied about my age, and I signed up. The man in charge of the gym was called Bernard, and he was from Barbados. He was in his late 60s and was so nice with me. He was essentially my personal trainer when I was in the gym.

School started again, and I was now in Year 6. It was only at this point that I was no longer behind after spending years working harder than everyone else to get where they were up to in the curriculum. I had a new teacher, and we called her Mrs E. She was an amazing teacher, and everyone who was in her class remembers her. I would say that she was the fairest teacher that I ever had. I used to sit on her table with two or three other friends, and she would always be there to help.

While writing this book I spoke to Mrs E, and here are the things that she can remember about me when I moved schools. The first thing that she could remember was me joining the school a few weeks before we broke up for the summer. There was a play at the end of the year for the Year 6 class, and some Year 5s would help. Mrs E's partner in crime, Mrs B – who was a teaching assistant – tried her best to get me to join in with the play, but I wasn't going to. She said that I was assertive from a young age and knew what I wanted. Mrs E also said that I worked hard, never gave up, appreciated any help and was respectful and kind. When we were doing difficult work, Mrs E would print off a check sheet, and when I had ticked everything off on the list, I would tell Mrs E, 'I've nailed it.'

Another thing that she could remember was how my disability never stopped me from doing anything. One day, I told Mrs E to repeatedly look at my hand. She did not know what I was going to say next. I then pointed out the disparity between the size of my left and right hand. I then told her that my right hand was bigger because I did all my work with it and started laughing. One thing that she noticed was how supportive my mum was. She said my mum would always be in my corner and encourage me to not let my disability beat me. Mrs E also said that when it was my turn to do the leavers' play, I took an active role and was dancing. The last thing Mrs E mentioned to me was that I got myself stuck into the canoeing that we did when we went to the Conway Centre for our end-of-year residential trip.

I remember finishing primary school at 3pm and then going to the gym, getting changed in the toilets there into the gym clothes that I took to school with me. We started with the very basics, doing sit-ups and the weight of the barbell on the bench press. After months of practice, I had weight on the barbell and was doing weighted sit-ups along with other exercises. I did not do many other exercises because I was too young to use the other equipment, even when I lied about my age. In the limited exercises that I was doing, Bernard commented how strong I was at 13 years old. It was at this point I spilled the beans and told him that I was actually only 11 years old.

We all went to Mallorca for a week away during the first half-term holiday after I got into Year 6. I missed the last day of term to get there. I was hoping that I would not be given the homework that was going to be given out on the last day, and I wasn't given it on the day before so that was good. We flew from Manchester Airport early in the morning and got into the hotel just after lunch. It boggled my mind how we had flown to a different country and were chilling by the pool just in a matter of hours.

The holiday was great; we didn't do anything spectacular, however, because my mum was pregnant with my sister. My mum would have a siesta and wasn't allowed to drink, but Graham was. He had toothache so was getting drinks down him to numb the pain. This was where I was introduced to vodka slushies, and he gave me my own. At the start of the first night, we sat outside next to the pool table. So we had a few games, and I was hooked. I couldn't do the standard guide with my left hand, so we experimented how I could use my left hand. We found putting my palm on the table and lifting my first two fingers while they stayed on the table worked, and I could shoot in a straight line. Graham then coached me through how to play a game of pool and what the rules are, and Fred joined in, even though he was only six. The tables were not maintained, and we may as well have been playing on a hill. That did not bother me, as I was playing Graham and trying to beat him. At the end of the day, the table was only there for fun. Me and my brother would spend hours at the pool table instead of being in the swimming pool. We kept begging our parents for money so that we could keep having games. When we were starting to get a little better, it was time to go home. When we got home, there was a parcel on the floor, and it was heavy. It was from my new primary school, which had posted the homework to my house that I thought I had missed. Being on my holiday and not knowing about it, I didn't have a lot of time to get it all done, but I did.

Me and my two younger brothers were 'given' a lot of things by our old next-door neighbour: things like suits he had found from the charity shop that were the right size. At the time, I didn't think anything of it. One day, I was told that I was getting a few days off school because we were going somewhere where something special was going to happen. In the car, me and Fred were guessing what the special thing was, but we weren't close at all. I wondered why my mum had her hair all done up, and then we pulled over at Lancaster services and were told that my mum and Graham were getting married. I was then asked to be best man. They were getting married at Gretna Green in Scotland, and no one knew except us. That was why my mum had started running and going to the gym. It was so that she would fit into her wedding dress. It was that night that they got married and I gave the rings out. Graham was now my stepdad, but he was still my dad anyway in the first place.

At the start of 2016, my sister was born, and she was named May, not because she was born in May but because that was the name of my great-grandmother. She was actually born in March. My mum had her at home. I woke up early one morning with our dogs scratching at the door trying to get out of my room. They were in my room because the midwife was scared of dogs, so we had to keep them out of the way. Graham was up and down the stairs and dropped me and my brother off at school. I then met my sister after I came back from school.

My mum had my sister at home like she had always wanted, but that did not keep her out of hospital, thanks to me. Three days after May was born, Graham took me, Fred and Joe for a bike ride. While I was getting my bike out, I managed to fall over it and chin myself on the handlebars because I lost my balance and tripped over my left foot. I cut my lip in the shape of my handlebars and chipped my front tooth. My mum was driving to Tesco, taking my sister out for the first time, and Graham phoned her saying not to panic but that I had cut my lip. When she came back and looked at what I had done to myself, she freaked out after Graham tried to keep me calm. So, we went off to hospital, and I had butterfly stitches and a tetanus shot. The tetanus shot hurt the most, as it was aching for the rest of the week. That's the story of how my mum went to hospital after having a baby at home. This is also how I acquired scar #2 on my chin. It's here to stay.

In Year 6, I started to play rugby for the school team. I enjoyed rugby, but we mostly did training and didn't play very many matches. Saying that, I did play at the Warrington Wolves' stadium and was on Sky TV. Unlike football, I wasn't going to keep my glasses on while I trained. I still needed to see, so the solution to my problem was to get contact lenses. I went to the optician, and even though I was young, they let me have contact lenses. Before you can take them home, you need to prove that you can put them in and take them out safely. I was a little nervous to do this because I didn't know whether I was going to be able to do it. I sat down and was trying to balance the lens on my finger. The opticians recommend that you use both hands, and I struggled. After 10 minutes of poking myself in the eyes, I was able to use both hands to put them in – I didn't put them in the conventional way that they recommended. After passing the test, I took them home and could wear them when I went to rugby training. I stopped wearing them shortly after, as I would only wear them when I was doing rugby, which I stopped when I left primary school.

There were only three rooms in my house, and Graham had to chop the end of the biggest room and create a fourth. As the eldest of four siblings, I have always offered a helping hand to my brothers and sister, as we are a big family. It's actually really funny being the big brother, as I can watch my siblings do the stupid stuff that I did when I was younger.

When I was in Year 6, my brother Joe was three. My mum brought Joe to pick me up from school. When he got out of the car, he ran to a motorbike on the side of the road – someone had just got off it. Joe jumped on it, started it up and was rev bombing it. I could hear the bike from the playground. Safe to say that my little brother was, and still is, a gangsta. It was also around this time that Joe learnt how to ride a bike, but he was a little shaky. When he fell off, he would copy what the Purple Helmets used to do. The

Purple Helmets were a group of people who rode motorbikes and clowned about trying to do stunts. They would imitate the Royal Signals (White Helmets) Display Team very poorly. Joe used to copy the Purple Helmets' signal – you would hold your crotch and have a hand on your head.

It was that same day when I saw someone from school on a pogo stick and thought, *I want to be able to do that*. I asked him for a go, and I couldn't even get on it without falling off. I was annoyed at how easy he made it look, so I decided that I needed to get one. When I got one, I practised in the back garden on the concrete. At first, I was scared because I didn't want to hurt myself, but eventually, I just did it. To begin with, I couldn't even stay on it, but the more and more I practised, the better I got, and eventually, I could stay on it and go where I wanted to. After a while, this got boring, and I needed to challenge myself again so decided to see if I could do it with no hands. Just like when I first started, I was scared when I tried it for the first time. I fell off, but I stayed on my feet, and from then on, I knew I could catch myself when I fell off. With a little practice, I was comfortably able to do it with no hands. I can only do this because I decided I needed to do it, as someone else was doing it.

At the end of Year 6, I did my SATS and then waited to go into my first year of high school. I had a look round the high school with the entire class as well as a few other classes that were going to go there the following year. This was to get our fingerprints on the system so we would be able to buy food with no hassle on the first day. We then had a quick look around the school before we had to get the school bus home. As I have a disability, there was another day that I could go and see the school to ask any questions that I might have. I went to the high school that day, not to ask questions but to get out of doing some work at my primary school. On that day, I had a better look round the school and saw what it was like when everyone was changing class. That didn't bother me in the slightest.

Before I left, a teacher from pastoral support got my name and said that I would get a lift pass when I next came in. In preparation for high school, I filled in a form online that I printed off and could give to a teacher if they asked what was wrong with me or how my disability affected me. I didn't do this, as I was shy about telling people what was wrong with my left side. Instead, I thought it was easier to think about what I would have to say once and put that down on paper so I would save my breath.

During the summer holidays, the new football team started to get boring for me, as I was with the foundation team because I was really not old enough to be in the older team. It just was not challenging me enough, and I found it easy. I was used to playing with people my own age on a mainstream team. That was challenging, as I had a disadvantage, but I enjoyed it more than being in the new team.

The last straw for me was when one of the parents congratulated me for walking down four concrete steps with a handrail by myself. I was congratulated for doing something that I did every day for years and that required no extra thought. For me, it felt like telling a chef well done for making beans on toast. It felt like a very condescending remark; that person had such a limited view of my potential. I'd had enough and quit that team. I tried to join my original team, but it had folded. That was the end of football for me.

During the summer holidays, I went to the children's hospital and the doctor that I was under at the time said, "Well I can tell someone has been wearing their splint since the last time I saw them". My mum was quick to tell the doctor that I wasn't using my splints and may as well throw them in the bin. He pulled a face of disgust and disbelief. Looking back, it seems that he was set in his ways and all he knew was the protocol to follow. My mum told him the reason that my walking was better was because I was keeping active and was not growing at the time.

On the first day of high school, Graham dropped me off on his motorbike, and the head teacher asked if I was going to turn up on that every day. I explained it was only for the first day and going forward I would be getting the school bus. I found which form I was in, but little did I know, I was in the form with some of the kids with the worst behaviour the school had ever seen, never mind just in my year. I can’t remember much about my first day at school, so it must have been alright. The only thing was that I didn’t know what to do at break and dinner. I enjoyed the new lessons, as they were new and interesting; we were learning things that I had never thought about before. I paid good attention to what I was getting taught and soaked it up like a sponge.

Twelve to fourteen years old

At home, I liked drumming and was getting good at it, but I wasn't big into it like my brother was, and I was getting shown up by him. Our room had a decent amount of space, but with a drum kit, we didn't have much room. As I slowly stopped using the drums and not having much space in my room, it was decided that the drum kit was to be kept at my gran's house in the spare room. It was nice to have the extra room, but I did miss being able to have a bash on them now and then. The drum teacher would come round to my gran's to give Fred a lesson, and I joined in now and then. My brother was getting to a level where he was going to need a drummer who was renowned for his drumming in a band. This didn't last long, however, because my brother also stopped playing the drums regularly and would only play when he was having a lesson, which is not the best. This meant that he wasn't taking it seriously enough for the help that he was getting, which in turn meant that he stopped playing the drums, as he didn't practise enough.

When my brother started to have lessons at my gran's house, I thought that I would give the guitar a go. I think that the drums weren't appealing to me, as they aren't recognisable in songs, and many of them have the same beat. On a regular guitar, you use your right hand to strum and left hand to change notes. This was no good for me, as my left hand wouldn't make the shapes it needed to make the right sounds. Graham was able to string the guitar the opposite way so I could use my right hand to change notes. I then found a guitar teacher who started with me and got me to do the basic songs, but early on, my fingers started bleeding. Although I was using my right hand to create the different notes, I still had to use my left hand to pick the strings. I could do it, but it was almost robotic because my hand was shaking, as that movement was intricate for me. I did this only for a few months, as I found it hard from the start, but I packed it in when my teacher introduced me to different strumming patterns in order to play more songs. Strumming patterns are important because they make songs sound different, and some songs sound wrong if they are not used. These strumming patterns added an extra layer to playing the guitar that I had to think about, and it was just getting too hard for me to do. If I had known what I know now – if you do something long enough, you will achieve your goal – I wouldn't have given up.

At school, there was a person who brought a Rubik's Cube in, and I thought that it was amazing how he could solve it in front of me – and others did, too. Other people would scramble it up for him. It wasn't just the standard Rubik's Cube that he was able to do either; he was able to do an octagonal cube. I started to slowly become friends with him and would spend my break and lunch with him and his friends from the local area and his primary school.

My boxing coach worked at the local supermarket, and I would see him there when I went shopping with my mum. He would ask when I was next going to attend and give me words of encouragement. I enjoyed doing boxing and did it for quite a few months, but I quit for four reasons. The first reason was that I was getting too old to be doing the Little Rockys class. The second was that I was finding the workouts repetitive, and therefore, they were not as fun as they used to be. The third reason was that I wanted to try and learn how to play the guitar. The last reason was that my mum had my little sister and could not take me to all these places while looking after her, so something had to give. It was boxing.

The biggest thing that I can remember from Year 7 was the difference between where I lived and where the people near school lived. The area that my high school was in was a posh area, and everyone there had everything branded, and the few odd people from where I lived stood out – not because we were scruffy, but because we couldn't afford the same phones and the same expensive shoes.

To travel to and from school, I got the school bus. kids living in the local area could get a bus pass for the year that cost £50, but the kids outside the area had to pay £1.50 each way. I am a few hundred metres out of the area that would allow me a bus pass. It was closer to walk to the bus stop than it was to the school closest to me with the bad reputation. My mum even tried seeing if throwing the disabled card in would work, but it didn't.

When I was in Year 1, there were some people in Year 6 who remembered me in my wheelchair when I broke my leg. They ended up going to the same high school as me and still remembered who I was – while they were in Year 11. They used to save me a seat at the back of the bus, so I was always guaranteed a seat.

I struggled to make friends in school because of where I lived and the fact that I did not really feel like I fitted in anywhere. This, however, did not stop me going round to a friend's house from primary school. There was me and another person at his house this particular day. All was going well, and we were on the trampoline trying to avoid a bouncing ball. The ball kept going over a low, spiky fence (my hip height) into the neighbour's garden. My friends jumped over the fence to get the ball, and I was in awe because they made jumping over the fence look easy. The ball went over again, and it was my turn to get over the fence. My friends were pushing me to get the ball even though I was reluctant, as I didn't want to hurt myself. In a state of paralysis, I was thinking about trying to jump over the fence, and then the penny dropped. I thought I couldn't do it because of my left side. My friends then started to get frustrated, as they thought I was being lazy and didn't want to get the ball. I got all emotional because I realised that I would not be able to do what my friends made look easy. I thought, *I should be able to do that but can't*. I nearly started to cry, and my friends then quickly became very understanding, but it was too late: I was going home. I managed to hold the tears back until I got out the house and was on my way home. On my way home, I was crying but was trying my hardest to stop, as I thought it was a trivial reason to get upset over. By the time I got back home, I had pulled myself together. My mum knew that I was upset and asked me what was wrong. I had a go at her and was very defensive. My mum was then going to bollock me, as she was only trying to help, so I told her why I was upset.

Year 7 for me was a year spent trying to figure out what I liked and what I wanted to do in my spare time, but it didn't go very well. This changed after the summer holidays, when in Year 8 at high school, a spokesperson from the Air Cadets came in to tell us what we could do if we joined. I remembered being really interested, as he said that I would be able to shoot guns, fly planes, do first aid and go on weekends away. I lived in one area and went to school in another; this meant that the spokesperson was representing the squadron for the school's area. This also meant that other people who were interested would not end up in the same squadron as me – or so I thought.

Where I lived was in the middle of three squadrons, but the one that was easiest to get to was not the one near school, so I would be joining a new group on my own. My parents were more than happy that I wanted to join the cadets, but the only catch was that the squadron was not exactly close. Anyway, I went down to the squadron for the first time, and it was really quiet and not like the spokesperson said it would be.

They introduced me to everyone and showed me the basics of how drill works. My parents came up with the idea that I could ask a friend from my old primary school (he was called Joel, and I had kept in touch with him) whether he wanted to join, so his parents and mine could share the lifts. He agreed, and from then on, me and my friend went down every Tuesday and Thursday.

As I went down more, I started to understand that we weren't doing everything the other squadrons were doing, just because of the low numbers that we had. To help with this, the squadron did a recruitment; this brought many other kids who lasted a few months, but only one or two stayed. This was because the kids were treating cadets as a youth club where they liked the idea of shooting guns etc. but didn't like the high levels of discipline that were needed to be in a squadron – for example, cleaning up at the end of the night.

The first event that I did was Remembrance Sunday. I did not have my uniform yet, so I went in my school uniform. We met at the squadron first before we took the minibus to the start of the march. I can't really remember much about being at the march; I guess I was concentrating on getting it right. However, looking back at the videos of us, I was shocked at the quality of the marching, as most of the recruits were not in time with the cadets in uniform.

I was then shown how to look after shoes and uniform; this was the first step to getting my own uniform. I practised polishing my school shoes and keeping them in good nick. The only piece of clothing that you have to buy is the shoes, and everything else is borrowed. I bought a pair of leather RAF shoes and polished them up and turned up to squadron in them, and my commanding officer (CO) was happy at what he saw. This is when I got measured up for my uniform. I did not get my uniform straight away, as the suppliers of uniforms changed the material of the clothes and had to make more. This meant that there was a backlog of orders. In the end, I got my uniform, but some of it was old and some of it was way too big, so I had to have it altered. One winter night, I brought all my uniform home in a bin bag with my name on it. After getting the uniform altered, I was able to go to the squadron in my uniform. This was when I finally felt like I was part of something, as I looked proper.

Nothing really happened at school in Year 8 except picking my GCSE options for Year 9. There was an options evening at school where each subject would try and sell themselves and show you the content that you would go over. In Year 8, I was in set two for science out of eight sets and wasn't allowed to pick triple science if I wanted to – it was a good job that I did not want to pick that anyway. I didn't pick subjects that would help me get a specific job because I didn't have a clue what job I wanted so picked what I enjoyed doing most. The options that I ended up picking were geography, computer science, design and technology and business, which was new to me, and I thought I would try. It may look like picking my options in Year 8 when I was 13 wasn't the best for me, but it actually was one of the best things that happened for me at school.

Summer 2018. The first taste of work that I had was washing my gran's and uncle's cars on the weekend. It was one good job in the summer. I would be in the sun drinking lemonade and washing the cars with cold, soapy water. It was a pleasant way to spend the morning. I would earn £5 per car. A good thing about this job was that it wasn't very physical; there was no heavy lifting, and I wasn't doing it for long. This meant that the job I had washing cars on the weekend was not giving me adverse effects on my left side throughout the week. It was nice to have this extra money. This job that I had at 13 happened because my gran wanted me to instil a little bit of work ethic in me from a young age.

Also in the summer of 2018, I went to the NABD rally – or the National Association of Bikers with Disabilities rally. If you don't know what it is, it is basically where you ride to a field and set a tent up and drink all weekend while you listen to music. Obviously, I didn't ride there, as I wasn't old enough, and I didn't drink either because I was only 13. I did camp there, however, and did listen to the music. When me and my family got there, we all struggled to put up the six-man tent that we had. After struggling for half an hour, a kind person who was already half drunk came to help, and we eventually got it up. It was a good weekend – plenty of things to do and plenty of stalls to look around. The best thing that happened was when my sister decided that she wasn't walking anymore and sat on the ground. We tried walking off to see if she would follow, but it didn't work. After 10 minutes, we sat at a table where we could still see her. Forty minutes passed, and she didn't budge. A man asked if starting a trike would work to get her moving, so we gave that a try, and when he revved it up, she came running over crying. The rally was good, as it showed me how they can modify bikes so people will be able to ride them if needed. The modifications include fitting adapted controls or changing the controls around. For example, people who have limited use in their feet may have a hand operated gear shifting system fitted.

At the end of Year 8, I was getting picked on at school. The group of friends that I was in were the outcasts. I wouldn't have thought of myself as an outcast, as I thought that there were no people who had the same interests as me, but no one would have spoken to me otherwise, so I joined in with them. It wasn't just me that was getting picked on; the entire group picked on each other, and it was banter. However, there was one person who was doing the exact same as the other people within my group but in a much more personal way. I knew the difference between not what you do but how you do it. I will call this person doing this to me Harrison.

The people that I spent my time with weren't bullies; in fact, some of them were the polar opposite. This group of people formed because we didn't like school and would dare each other to do stupid things like throwing a bottle of water in the air and seeing whose head it would land on. This was to make break and lunch go faster so I would be in lessons concentrating. Another thing that we would do is trip each other up, but Harrison would only do it to me, and he did it maliciously. On the other hand, there was a person who was trying to get me to join the gym and get me to come to his karate dojo.

This person in particular said that I could come to the gym with him after school. I did join the gym, and I didn't know what exercises to do, but he showed me what would be best for me to do in there. For what was at the gym, it was expensive and it was after school, and this meant that I would miss the school bus. With no other way home, I would have to be picked up. For that reason, going to the gym didn't last long, but he recommended me to join his karate, which wasn't too far from where I lived. He said that karate wasn't the best martial art for me, as it has a factor of strength. With half of me not being as strong as the other half, it stuck in my mind, and I researched the most suitable martial art for me to do: it was Brazilian jiu-jitsu. I looked at the closest place that taught this, and it was way too far away and also too expensive. I then forgot about martial arts but know in hindsight I should have taken the offer from my friend to join his karate dojo anyway.

Going to the gym and looking into martial arts were really the closest experiences that I had to physiotherapy while in high school. This is because I saw my physio twice at school in my five years there. I didn't get physio at home either, but I would go to the children's hospital to see how I was and if my condition was bad enough that it required real help. Otherwise, I was left to my own devices to manage and improve my condition.

While all of this was happening at school, there were also plenty of things happening at cadets. For months and months, I was working towards the first badge, which allowed you on weekends away. As the numbers of my squadron were low and another squadron in the area had low numbers, the wing commander decided to merge the two squadrons. The CO of the other squadron was to be the CO of the merged squadron. This was because my CO was going to be promoted if he went to a different squadron with more cadets. The other squadron changed location and moved to our building, but to make it fair, parade nights of the other squadron were on their original nights, which were a Monday and a Wednesday. The other squadron had many other cadets and had many people in green coveralls, as they were recruits. The new CO tested every cadet from our squadron with a basic drill test. If I could not pass the test, I would have my uniform taken away from me. I hadn't had my uniform long and didn't want it taken off me. I passed and kept my uniform, which was a weight off my shoulders.

The first night of every month, the squadron had a uniform inspection. Up until now, my mum was ironing my uniform, so I decided that I needed to practise doing it myself. I spent two hours getting my uniform ready for inspection. After the inspection, the CO read the scores that we got out loud.

Before he did that, though, he said, 'It looks like some people have not bothered with the inspection tonight.'

I thought to myself that it couldn't be me, as I had spent a long time getting my uniform ready. He then announced my score, and if I can remember, I got four out of ten. After saying my score to the squadron, he said it looked like I had ironed my uniform with a brick. This made me so angry, as I had put literal hours into my uniform for it to be insulted. I don't think what my CO did was bad, as I needed to hear the harsh truth. Hearing the harsh truth would help me improve, and I asked my mum for the best way to iron the creases into my pants and shirts. She showed me, and after practising ironing my uniform before each parade night, I started to be one of the top scorers on my uniform.

I liked cadets more with extra people, as we could do more activities. With a weekend away, my new CO focused on getting everyone in uniform and all of us getting our first-class badge. Our CO hosted a day at squadron where we would fill in a booklet full of answers to be awarded the badge. Before the squadrons merged, the old CO took me and my friend Joel through the majority of the booklet, so on the day of first-class completion, I only had to fill in the last three sections, but I had to wait until the end of the day to be given the information. My friend Joel, however, was on holiday and couldn't complete the booklet required for the first-class badge.

With everyone at squadron having the first-class badge – or higher – except my friend, there was then a pass-out parade. This is similar to the military when you have a pass-out parade to celebrate finishing training. This was to celebrate getting our uniform, performing drill to a basic standard and getting our first badge, making us basic cadets who could take part in activities. At our pass-out parade, our parents were able to come at the end of the night, where we got into a squad and the CO said a few words about us and what we were going to be doing.

After this happened, Joel decided that he was going to move to a different squadron, where they were doing more activities. That squadron's parade night was the same as mine. One Monday night, I asked Joel if he was going to see whose parents were going to take us. He told me that he was ill and wasn't going that day. No problem – I went there myself and enjoyed the night. Days later, he told me that he wasn't ill and had gone to look at another squadron. I then told one of the people who I knew at cadets what had happened. My CO overheard what I said and asked me why he did it, but I didn't have a clue.

Throughout the year, there would be multiple wing training weekends, and there was one coming up. As I passed first-class, the only activity that I could do was bushcraft. This was a good activity for my first weekend away, as it was about entertainment and was a chance for the new cadets to get a feel for weekends away. I got the kit list that I needed, and I packed my suitcase. I did not have to pack much, as I was in combats all weekend.

A few days before I left to go on this trip with the cadets, my mum did not feel well and was bedbound. She was in bed all day and was still ill and asleep when I left

As Graham was taking me to wing HQ, I started to get nervous, as I was going into the unknown. At the gate, a corporal asked to see my ID to get into the car park to get on the coach. As I sat down on the coach, my nerves started to calm, as there were many other people on there and I was sitting next to people from my squadron. We got to the army base and entered the gym, where we were told all the safety information. I was then shown to my bed and was left to feel at home until lights out.

The next day, we all got up early in the morning and had breakfast. We then went into the forest, where we were shown how to put a shelter up and had a go at it ourselves. We were walking through a field, and a key memory that I have from cadets was randomly falling into a ditch while speaking to a girl from my squadron. She found it really funny and asked if I was okay. She then helped drag me out of the ditch. From now on, I will call her Chloe. We had a game of hide and seek vs the staff. We were shown how people mark fields and search for objects. On the way back to the barracks, I was asked if I wanted to get into the minibus, as I had walked miles that day in high temperatures while wearing heavy combat gear. I was the only person allowed in the minibus if I wanted a lift back. I was happy to carry on walking, but there was one cadet who managed to get a lift back because she was begging. At night, I don't remember anything happening other than everyone ordering Domino's pizza. The next day, I packed my gear up and then cleaned the barracks and went home.

I didn't go straight home, though; I had a stop off at the hospital. The day after I left with the cadets, my mum went into hospital, as she was so ill. The doctor quickly discovered that she had sepsis and was struggling to get better. I turned up to the hospital in my combats because I didn't have time to get changed and was expecting to get some weird looks, but surprisingly, there were not that many people who noticed me in them – I must have been camouflaged. My mum said the doctor told her she if she had left it 12 to 24 hours longer before she went to hospital, her chances of survival would not have been good. This left Graham to look after me and my three other siblings. Graham is not a great cook, so we were eating plenty of beans on toast. It was only after my mum got out of hospital that I realised how ill she had been, and she told me that one in three people at her age who get sepsis die. It was also noted that she had high levels of potassium in her blood.

There was a weapons training day at the activity centre in our area. I did this and found it very hard. The weapon that I was using was only a single-shot rifle, but my left arm was barely able to keep the rifle up. I passed the weapons handling test and got the signature from the assessor that I needed to go shooting, which lasted six months. I didn't even shoot a live round that day.

Summer break then came round for me, and this six-week period was mainly filled with me playing on my Xbox and going to cadets twice a week, trying to get on courses and do new things. As I live a fair distance away from school, the people who I knew were all far away, and there were no buses to that area. This meant that it was very rare when I met someone out of school. For that reason, I didn't get too involved in what everyone was doing at school and kept myself to myself.

So I started doing boxing again, as it was something to do to keep me busy and was good for me. My brother also came with me, as he wanted to do something; he had nothing to do at that point in time. At one session, my coach said to me that my brother would make a good fighter because of his lazy style on the bag. Obviously, this lit a fire inside of me because in my head, that meant he was better than me. I tried to be 'the lazy' style, but my coach was telling me that I needed to work harder. I could not fathom how my brother was good at being lazy but I was not. This was when I decided that if I could not do the same, I would do the opposite. Every session, I would push myself 110 per cent. I would hit the bag until I couldn't hold my arms up anymore. I would try to complete circuits as fast as I could and keep my legs up on the leg holds longer than my brother. My coach asked me to do 20 burpees: this is when you go from a push-up position to doing a straight jump and back down again. I can remember trying to do them at the same pace as the amateur fighters and only being a few seconds behind them. I was pushing so hard that I felt sick after every session.

I kept myself to myself until we tried to do a new recruitment at cadets, so I went to the local youth club to see if anyone was interested. As soon as I got to the youth club, I realised that the type of people who went there would not fit in. This, however, didn't stop me going out every Friday to meet people for a little while. I would go and meet people I had never seen before, and they were all doing things like smoking weed and doing balloons (nitrous oxide). I wasn't interested and didn't join in with any of this, even though people would offer me some. After going for a few weeks, it got boring, so I stopped going, and that was the end of that.

At this time, there was a job going at a pet shop, covering for some staff while they were away. This was a perfect Sunday job for me to earn a bit of cash. They were looking for staff and someone warned us that the boss could be grumpy, but I thought that wasn't going to be too bad. At this job, I would clean out the reptile cages and give them fresh food and water, feed the fish, clean the tanks, clean up after the parrots and serve customers. The boss was grumpy and was so bad that he actually made other people on their first day leave, crying. One time after I finished up brushing, for example, I asked him if he wanted me to do anything else. He snapped at me, "Stop fucking asking me questions and leave me alone!" Where I struggled in this job was bagging the fish. I wouldn't have a problem catching the fish, but putting extra oxygen in the bag and tying the bag was where I struggled. When you bag fish, you need to fill the bag with pure oxygen for people to take them home. Tying the bag was hard for me, as my left hand does not have the strength or dexterity needed to hold a bag full of water and use an elastic band to tie the top of the bag. I would even stay at my gran's house when the rest of my family went to Wales so that I could be there for the pet shop to do my job. The pay was good when I started.

I then left because the original staff came back. A few months later, the boss phoned me back asking if I could do a few shifts, but he was offering less money, and I knew he was going to treat me badly like he did the first time, so I passed.

Later on in the holidays I had the best experience I had with the cadets. There was a week away at RAF Spadeadam. There were 20 of us, and many of us were from my squadron, as my CO was the head of the camp. The first reason that made it good was that we ate some of the best food in the RAF – military food is normally not the best. The next thing was that we had a building full of PlayStations and flight simulators made just for the cadets. It was a place where we could chill out when we weren't doing anything. Another thing that I liked about this was that my friend from high school who I will call Tom, from a different squadron, went as well.

As I arrived, I pretended to be a corporal. People figured out quite quickly that I was not one, but they called me corporal for the rest of the week. This quickly got out of hand with many field promotions: I was eventually Air Vice Marshal Corporal Rickman. We went on trips out to other RAF bases; one of them showed us what they did in air traffic control. We went to Hadrian's Wall and had a look around museums. I was managing the walking better than other people.

One day, we had a look at what the firefighters do. We all had a go at using the fire hose, trying to knock a traffic cone over. We then tried to find a way through a pitch-black building with obstacles, similar to the conditions that the firefighters face.

Everybody liked me that week, and I got on well with everybody as well. In fact, me and this sergeant became good friends. He had a bubbly personality, and it was infectious – we were always having a laugh. He even went as far as being my wingman and tried to get me a girlfriend. Chloe was on this trip away, and my friend was saying how cute me and her would be together. He then bigged me up in front of everyone. I thought about her being my girlfriend but knew nothing would come from it after the week away was finished. I lived far away from squadron, and she lived far away from squadron in the opposite direction. Essentially, she lived far, far away, and for that reason, I did nothing. Maybe the real reason was that I was nervous. Honestly, I am not sure what it was, as that was quite some time ago.

Except the visits to different RAF stations and the other activities that we did, there were little experiences that happened in the middle of everything we were doing. We had random room inspections, and I was lucky, as I cleaned the top of my locker by accident, scoring points. For 24 hours, I had to eat nothing but ration packs, and I didn't actually mind it that much, as I am not a picky eater.

At the end of the week, we did paper plate awards. There were many awards up for grabs like the best couple, the tidiest, the 'I'm fine' award and the best overall cadet award. I got two awards that week: I got an award for being an Air Vice Marshal and another award for being the best overall cadet, not that I am trying to brag or anything. With the trip being one week long, it was the right length, as towards the end, we were all ready to go home. On the way home, I was given a bottle of water and drank it all. It was only after I had drunk it all that I was told that we were travelling back without any stops. I regretted drinking that bottle of water straight away. Not long into the journey on the way home, I needed to go to the toilet and had to keep myself from making a mess for the rest of the three hours on the way back. When we finally got back, I jumped off the coach and left my stuff and was waiting at the door of wing HQ for the staff to open it. The staff didn't know what the code was, and I had to wait even longer. I finally got into the building and followed a cadet who knew the way round there to the toilets.

In the back end of 2018, we wanted to go away and spend time out of the house, so we decided to try camping. We borrowed a caravan and followed a family friend down to a field in Anglesey where he used to camp. We put the PW50 motorbike in the caravan and brought it down with us. We brought the motorbike with us because the campsite was a working farm that had a spare field with no rules. We loved the field that we were staying at, as we would do nothing all day except go on the bike and have a fire at night. The PW50 was now too small for me, but Fred could ride it, and Graham decided that Joe – who wasn't even five then – could have a go. It was so funny watching Graham run up and down the field chasing Joe on the bike. A couple of hours on the bike and Joe was doing laps of the field. He was fearless, and towards the end of the week, Graham had to restrict the bike because he was going flat out. We would also go to the beach for a change of scenery. Our family friend let me drive his van around the field, and my mum was in there with me and was cringing as I pressed the brakes but slid on the wet grass towards a stone wall. We liked the field that we stayed at, so we carried on going there when we could.

The first day of Year 9 finally came around after I'd seemingly waited so long for it. This was when my GCSE subjects started, and I realised how repetitive and tedious my new timetable was with only doing seven subjects multiple times a week. However, that did not stop me enjoying the content of these new lessons. I like learning, as it broadens the mind and puts things into perspective. Even so, I still thought break and lunchtime were a waste of time, and I couldn't stop myself mixing with people who were not the best for me. Harrison started to pick on me again, and it was constant this time. He started to throw stuff at me. One day, Harrison threw bolts at my head in maths and the teacher was in the room but somehow didn't see what was happening.

Next, he started to take some of my money off me so he could go to the shop and buy sweets. This would be my bus money, and that meant that over the course of the week, I wouldn't have enough money to get home. I used to use the little pocket money that I was given and the money from washing the cars that I got to cover the money that used to get taken from me. After every PE lesson, I would check my blazer pocket and count all my money because I got changed in the same room as Harrison. After one PE session, a £20 note was missing. I can't say for sure that it was Harrison, but with his track record of stealing my money, I think it was him. I had no bus money for the rest of the week and had to ask my mum for more. She was furious at me. I said it was my fault so she would not find out what was happening at school.

After a while, I was fed up of this happening and thought to myself, *Should I just hit him?*

At that point in time, I was one of the smallest kids in the year and this person was a lot taller, so the odds weren't in my favour. There was another thing that stopped me hitting him, even though I was close to doing it many times: I was still going to boxing at this point, so I did know how to throw a decent punch, but with the situation at home with me and Fred, I just let everything slip without fighting back. I was taught not to fight back when Fred started to annoy me and hit me. I just let it happen and let my mum or Graham deal with it.

Weeks after this started, something happened that I will always remember. Harrison held me by my bag and then dragged me across the floor around the school. It was from then on that I knew that something needed to change; I didn't change anything, the bullying carried on, and I kept it all to myself until two weeks later, when I just broke down. I broke down that day in particular because he had cornered me and stolen more money off me. I felt defenceless. For the rest of that week, I stayed off school while the teachers looked into what had happened. They then got my friends to write a report to see what they had to say. I thought that the other kids didn't like Harrison as well. That was more than true when I was told what they had put in the reports. They made him seem even worse than he actually was.

While I was off, the teachers were looking at the CCTV footage, trying to see where I was dragged across the floor. They said that they couldn't find anything, but it couldn't exactly be hard when I said it started at the start of lunch when I came out of a computer room. When Harrison was questioned about what he had done, it looked like a teacher had noticed how he was picking on me. After everything that had happened, he only got two days' isolation at my school and another day at another school. According to the policies written by school, his behaviour should have got him excluded.

Fourteen to sixteen years old

When I was 14, my parents thought that I was old enough to start babysitting for them. They only went to the local pub, which is a 10-minute walk away. My brother Joe was fine and easy to take care of, as he was five. My sister, May, was in bed before my parents went out of the house. This left my brother Fred. He didn't like that I was in charge of him, even though I wasn't asking anything of him. In fact, he would be deliberately difficult to see what he could get away with. It would be little things like me telling Joe he was not allowed in the back garden, so that was where Fred went. Obviously, that wasn't fair on Joe, so then I told Fred to come in, and then he started having a go at me. I dealt with this fine, but it didn't stop my parents from phoning me multiple times to make sure that I was okay. They even asked people on the street to intervene if I needed any help.

The first few times that I was looking after everyone, Fred would test me and would even phone my mum and Graham, saying that I was 'power hungry'. As I babysat more and more, he realised that I wasn't unreasonable and left me to deal with Joe and May, who were no problem anyway.

The start of Year 9 was when I stopped doing PE. A new person came to the school and joined the local rugby club – let's call him Jack. He was only small. Only a few weeks later, he was tackled and dislocated his hip in training. It was at the same time I had my toenail removed because of complications of how I walk. This meant that we were both not doing PE, and we got to know each other. The first thing that he made me realise was that it wasn't fair what the PE teachers were doing. It was the middle of winter, and we were in shorts and T-shirts while they were wearing coats, gloves and hats. Doing PE in the cold was not only unfair, but it was a major inconvenience for me as my hands were frozen, even with gloves on. It is known that people with the same condition as me can't use their hands when they are cold; I am no exception. In the changing rooms, I would ask my friend to do my top button, as

I couldn't dress myself because I was unable to bend my fingers (even on my good hand).

Every PE lesson, I would talk to Jack, and then I started to talk to him at lunch and break until we were basically not apart. It was good that he came to the school when he did, as I could hang around with him instead of the group with Harrison that was giving me a hard time. If we were in the same lesson, we would sit together and would always meet at the lunch queue. When we weren't at school, we were on the Xbox, talking online. I think that me and Jack got on so well because we both had the same interests and views at school. We were so bored at lunchtime that we would just walk entire laps around the school and go out of bounds because there was nothing else to do. We spent that much time together that multiple people asked if we were gay when we were just best mates.

Year 9 was a blur really for me, as I hated being at school. I only have memories of getting detentions for doing no work in class – which did not bother me, as I hated my breaks and lunches anyway – so I would just chill out in a classroom in a detention with my head on the desk. They weren't a punishment to me. I was doing no work in class, as we did a lot of revision, and I could retain the information from the subject being taught. The teacher could ask me a question and I would give the right answer. As I found the work mundane, I would just daydream instead. Originally, I was in set one maths, then got moved down to set two maths. I was getting the same scores as other people in set one but was moved down because of my behaviour. This bothered me, so I started behaving and wasn't moved back; this was when I completely gave up with school. My teacher said that it was okay if I didn't want to do the work, but I wasn't allowed to distract others. From then on, I just kept my head on my desk for the next four months, and the most I did in my maths lessons was write the date.

As I hated school, I liked doing things with my own time at home. One week, my uncle invited me to come along with him to the local pub quiz night. On Sunday nights, we would head down to the pub and play pool before the quiz started. This was the first time that I had played pool properly since I went to Spain when I was 11. The biggest thing was trying to find a guide that worked for me. My uncle would try and get me to use the most common guides, and we tested many things to see if we could get them to work for me. They weren't working for me, and I started to use my left hand the same way I did when I was in Spain. This was when I could start to focus on trying to pot the balls on the table. Every game that I had was painfully long because I was terrible. This meant that I would only have a couple of games before the quiz started each week. I wasn't very good at this either; the quiz highlighted that I didn't know any music at all. I enjoyed going to the pub on Sunday nights, but I stopped going when my uncle signed up to the Royal Navy. I stopped playing pool and didn't have anything to do in my week except cadets and boxing.

The icing on the cake with school was when Jack started to spend time with girls. We would be in a group of girls, and he would be speaking to them while they all ignored me. After a few weeks, he got himself a girlfriend and didn't want to know me anymore. Before this happened, he would go out of his way to find where I was at lunch, and the next minute, he pretended that I didn't exist. The only time that he spoke to me was when he wanted the answers to the geography homework. It was at that point I realised that he wasn't actually a good person. His girlfriend only lasted so long, however, and then he came looking for me at lunch again. It was at this point when I could not be bothered with him and went back to the people that I spent most of my time with at the start of school.

In the middle of all this happening, my little brother Joe became ill. Joe had chickenpox, and in rare cases, it can turn into pneumonia, which is what happened, but we didn't know. My mum knew that chickenpox should only last so long, and as he stayed ill, she took him to the doctor, but all they would say was that he was ill. After a week of being as sick as a dog, Joe was taken by my parents to A&E, and they were told that he was suffering from constipation.

Two days later, I woke up with paramedics coming through the door and my brother crying with a pain in his chest and blood coming out of his nose. Graham went in the ambulance with Joe, and my gran picked me, Fred, May and my mum up. We then stayed at my gran's, and my gran took my mum to hospital. This happened on a Friday night, and when I got up on the Saturday morning, my gran told me that Joe had pneumonia, which had also led to sepsis, but that he should be alright. When I asked my brother what had happened when he went to the hospital, he told me that he had had many blood tests and been given a walker. He was given a walker because he was struggling to stand and was falling over. Joe also told me that he was given ice cream and that was the best bit about hospital. At the time, I knew how severe Joe's condition could be, after something similar had happened to my mum. For this reason, I kept myself busy to distract myself. I would sit in front of the TV while polishing my cadet shoes.

Even though my gran was looking after us all, I was still going to cadets. I looked forward to going to cadets, as it was something that kept my mind busy. School also kept me busy, but I wasn't myself, and for that reason, they phoned home to see whether everything was okay. During this, Joe went to Alder Hey Children's Hospital for better care. He needed a chest drain to get the infection out of his lung, but they needed an X-ray before they could do this. The person that did the X-ray ticked the box for right lung instead of left lung, which was where a problem started. The doctor who did this should have known his left and right because he was missing an arm. After this happened, Joe needed another X-ray before he could have the chest drain in. They then kept delaying putting the drain in when he needed it.

I was watching Glastonbury on the TV, and my gran came in telling me that I could go and see Joe the following day. Graham picked me up the next day and took me, Fred and May to see Joe. When I saw Joe, he was playing a game on a tablet. His favourite word was 'no', and you could ask him anything and he would just say 'no'. When he was getting a good score on his game, the heartbeat monitor would start beeping, and the nurses would come in to turn it off. A few more days passed, and Joe was let out of hospital, but he was nothing but skin and bone, and it took months to get weight back on him.

It was roughly about this time also when I experienced favouritism in cadets, but I wasn't on the receiving end. When the squadrons merged, there were the people in the green coveralls; these were the other squadron's new recruits. Chloe got her uniform and the first-class classification at the same time as me. As she was a little older, she started her leading cadet classification earlier than me. This allowed her on a course that would make her eligible for corporal; as I wasn't doing the course, I wasn't. I started cadets almost a year before she did, but I wasn't even eligible for the promotion to corporal. The way that my CO structured my training meant that I wasn't allowed on a course that was needed for me to be promoted, but the other cadet was. This was done on purpose; the CO's favourite was Chloe, and other people – including herself – knew it. With me not allowed to go on the course, it meant that there was less competition for the promotion.

The next thing in my cadet career was that the squadron was trying to get a percussion badge by learning the drums. I found this near impossible, as you need to hold the drumsticks a certain way. It just was not working for me; this was when I came up with the idea of learning how to play the trumpet so I would also be able to get a music badge. This was one of the best ideas I have ever had. One of my officers could play the trombone and the bagpipes, so he said that I could come down early to have lessons. With my mum hearing about the news, she asked someone she knew if I could have a lesson because she played for the local band. This helped with my progress a lot. The first song that I played was the national anthem. I was told that there was going to be a squadron band and that I would be leading it; this never materialised either. I did really well with the trumpet, as I was nearly put in for my grade one after just seven months of practice.

On top of the favouritism that everybody saw, we were also promised there would be a band and other things that we would do, and none of it came to fruition. One of these promises was doing the Duke of Edinburgh Award. It took months to set our account up and figure out what we were going to do in order to receive the award. We then forgot about it and moved on to other things at squadron like being trained on air rifles for the range that was installed. For one reason or another, I was not able to complete the training.

This was where cadets went downhill for me, and I was telling my friends there that I was thinking about quitting because it was getting boring. This was when I decided to have a look at the squadron my friend Joel had moved to. On the way down to his squadron, he told me that I hadn't picked a good night to come down because we were unpacking a minibus. I got there, and they were doing drill differently from how I was used to doing it. My friend's CO then introduced himself and also told me that I hadn't picked a good night to come down. I will admit the night wasn't that exciting, but it wasn't terrible. The only thing that I didn't like was the other cadets. They were too prim and proper for me, and they were just stuck-up in my eyes. They were too posh for me, and that was the deal-breaker.

As I was getting a little older and had no one to share lifts with to get to cadets, I was told to take the bus to squadron if I wanted to carry on going. I started to get the bus and had to leave five minutes early at the end of the night to catch the only bus home. This was a problem because my CO liked to overrun at the end and talk about what he wanted to do. This meant that I would get the next bus, which was at 10.25pm, and it would be 11pm by the time I got home. That was the problem, with just getting home.

The problem going to cadets was a mixture of two things. It was how much time I was spending there and how much time I had for myself. As I was going to squadron early for my music lessons, I needed to get out before the rush-hour traffic to get there on time. To get to squadron on time, I would get home from school and have a shower and then put my uniform on. I would then very carefully eat my tea and try not to get it on my uniform. I would be out the door by 5.30pm. I would then be getting back at 11pm if I missed the first bus, and I was doing that twice a week. That is not too bad, but I was also busy when I didn't go to squadron. I would spend a couple of hours a day after parade night, ironing and polishing my shoes to make them look as good as new.

Back at school towards the end of the year, Harrison was still with that group of friends, but enough time had passed to where the storm had blown over. In fact, me and Harrison got along. When I started to see these people again, there was one new person, and he was fat. That was Harrison's new target. I could see the same happening to him as what happened to me, but I just kept out of it; I didn't want to reignite the flame again. The other people also noticed what was happening and tried to help, but it was too easy to pick on his new target. Before I knew it, Year 9 was over, and it was the summer holidays.

At the start of the holidays, we bought a cheap, nasty 125cc pit bike that we could take camping with us. The PW50 was automatic, and this new bike was manual, so I had to learn how to use gears. Fred was still in primary school, and the new pit bike was too big for him, so Graham had to lower it, and he could just about reach the ground with his tiptoes. We then went camping and brought the new bike as well as the PW50 for Joe.

This was where my disability really could have affected my ability to ride a bike. I knew that if I could not get to grips with the gears, riding in the future would be so much harder, but not impossible. Me and my brother, on the way down to the campsite, had a game of rock, paper, scissors, and he won. We got to the site and set up the caravan. The pit bike then fired up, and my little brother got the first go. Graham told him how to operate a geared bike with the basics of the biting point on the clutch and changing gears. It was then my turn, and Graham showed me through the basics of a geared bike as he had my brother because we both knew how to ride smaller automatic bikes. I had my go, and I managed to set off and change a few gears. The ride was slow and jumpy. I had to stop because my left hand got tired of pulling in the clutch lever. This was because the clutch was very stiff.

To help with this, Graham showed me how to change up a gear

without the clutch so I would pull the lever in less. This eased the stress on my left hand, and I could focus on my downshifts. On every shift, I talked my way through it. In-down-off-go. This was to get the coordination of moving my legs and hands in the right order. Eventually, my gear changes became quicker, as it slowly became muscle memory. My brother took to it rather quickly, but I was still struggling. I could have been disheartened because he was better, but I knew that he would be better than me because I started with a disadvantage. Eventually, I became just as good as my brother on the new bike. It was at this point I started using the clutch to change up the gears. Just like learning to ride a push bike, I gave myself a massive blister across my left hand because I was moving my hand about to use the clutch.

Our family friend came down later that day. The morning after, he was recovering from a session, and Fred got on the pit bike and was running up and down the field. Our family friend thought that it was Graham riding the bike because it sounded that smooth. The competition between me and my brother was high to see who was the best. My brother was a smoother rider, but I was more of a daring rider, and I wasn't afraid to use all that the poor bike had to offer, which wasn't too much anyway.

Like the year before, me and my family went to the NABD rally, but this time we did not go in a tent but a caravan. I can't remember much about going the second time, as it was similar to the first time that I went. There were three differences that I can recall. The first was that my mum asked my grandad whether he wanted to go or not. He hadn't been to the NABD before but didn't go because he wanted to go with his friends, and they were busy. The next thing that I can remember was my sister pole dancing at the front of the beer tent at three years old. Next was looking after Joe and May in the caravan while my parents stayed out.

The last trip I went on with the Air Cadets was to the National Aerospace camp. I was banking on this trip to be a good one so I would stay in cadets. At this camp, there were 300 cadets and two others from my squadron; Chloe and her friend, who I will call Haley. We stayed at one barracks and went on a coach to get to another RAF base that had gliders. The logistics with the coaches were so bad that a hashtag started trending on the camp's Facebook group called #justwaitingfor. We would keep ourselves busy on the Facebook group, as we were sometimes waiting up to three hours for a coach to pick us up.

On this week away, everyone was guaranteed to go up in the air and earn our blue wings. I did many things, such as building a pair of wings that we put on a small wooden glider to see how far it would travel, having a go at robotics, going on the flight simulator, going on an air traffic control simulator, going to a museum, taking an engine apart – and I even sat in a new F-35 cockpit. Don't get me wrong: I found all the experiences interesting and enjoyed being away. One thing that I did not do was go in the air, however. Guaranteed to go in the air but didn't. They were even running a course for a badge that I didn't have, but they wouldn't let me do it.

At the end of the week, though I got my flying certificate saying that I earned my blue wings, I found out that I was one of the three out of 300 who did not go in the air. This was when I thought, if one more letdown happened, I was leaving the cadets.

The only saving grace on that week away was the fact that there were people I knew. On a week away such as this, I learnt that the people there are also another factor that either makes or breaks your experience. For some reason, I thought that everyone was one of two types of people. They were odd bods or the big 'I am'. Instead of trying to get involved with these people in my own time, I used to spend my time speaking to Chloe. Haley was off chatting to everyone and would just leave Chloe. Sometimes, I would go to find her, and sometimes she would come to find me. It was easier said than done in a group of 300 people. We talked about squadron politics and life.

When I got back to squadron, I handed my certificate to my CO so that I could get my blue wings without ever going in the air. I then completed the criteria for another badge, one that I did in my own time, and I waited months for the pair of them, which in the end I did not get.

The last thing that I was banking on to make cadets better was being next in line to be promoted. After having to do a personal statement, a presentation in front of 30 people and an interview, I was promoted. I remember a cadet asking if I was surprised about being promoted. I just thought to myself, *I am not surprised; I should have got it earlier.* I then went to cadets a few more times until I realised being promoted did not make it better; it actually made it worse. I lost interest and stopped going almost immediately. That was the end of cadets. Since I was learning how to play the trumpet for cadets, I couldn't see the point of playing anymore, so I quit doing that as well.

The start of Year 10 was nothing special. I still wasn't doing my work and was counting the days left until I could leave. The only thing that happened was between me and Jack. Since he betrayed and used me when he got a girlfriend and came back when they fell out, I didn't have anything to do with him. Over the summer holidays, he wanted to speak to me online, but I would ignore him. When we got back to school, it was awkward between me and him, as we would sit next to each other in many classes and you could feel hostility in the air. I was fed up with us sitting next to each other and not speaking. All I did was put Jack's book on his table for him, and that stopped the awkwardness and the hostility that we both felt. We did talk to each other now and then, but it was nothing like how it was in Year 9. I was more than happy with this and wanted it to stay that way after what had happened.

In March, Prime minister Bozzer told us that we weren't allowed out of the house, and lockdown happened. I loved it at the beginning. I would play on my Xbox with people from school all day, every day, for weeks. My school managed to get the work online, but my parents told me that I didn't have to do it when it was first accessible. After the first five weeks or so, my parents decided that I needed to do my online work, but I didn't want to do it, as I thought it was all revision. For the next few weeks, I was forced to do my work, and so was Fred. We half-did the work every day until Graham found out that I wasn't doing it properly and it wasn't even that hard in the first place. He then turned the internet off until one o'clock every day, until the work was done. Me and my brother didn't only have to do the work set that day, but we had to do all the work we missed and redo the work we had half done. I was at a laptop for six hours a day for months while I caught up with all the work. My brother, on the other hand, was at a laptop for six hours a day for months like me but was stalling doing his work, so it took him even longer to complete it all. I was right: all the work was just revision, except the work from geography – geography had new lessons I had to do.

After I did my work, I would go back on my Xbox, and when the weather got better, I lived in the garden. There was a rusty old BMX in the shed, and I thought that I would strip it down and repaint it. I had to sand all the rust and old paint off before I could do anything else. Next, I used cheap primer for the paint to stick on, and the paint was just peeling off. I spent hours sanding the bike back down again before I used better primer and the paint stayed on. Another thing that we did was have a get-together with most of the people on the street at the front of our house for the 75th anniversary of VE Day. My mum made food, and we were all having a drink – socially distanced, of course.

In the middle of lockdown, I finally got bored of doing the same things every day, but I carried on doing them, as I didn't know what else I should do. If I was to do anything, I should have started running for exercise or learnt a new skill. I didn't do anything like that and carried on playing on my Xbox and got used to feeling bored. As I was in Year 10, I was given a date where I could go in school for three hours on a Monday. As I was playing catch-up with my work, I finally did all the unfinished work three weeks before I was going back into school for half a day a week.

This was when the rules were changing, and nobody knew where they were up to with what they were allowed to do. We saw an opening to go to Wales to go camping, so that is what we did. The farmer's field that we camp at had a family living there, and their family dog was pregnant. This dog would run into our caravan and would beg for food. It was close to my mum's birthday, and she decided that she wanted one of the pups. Graham didn't want another dog but warmed to the idea when my mum come up with the name Metisse. There is a motorbike company called Rickman Metisse, which makes a bike frame that can fit multiple engines. It also means 'lady of mixed heritage', which these pups are. The mum is a whippet cross greyhound, and the dad is a Presa Canario mastiff.

Two days after we went home, the pups were born, and we just had to wait until we could get a pup. Two weeks later, we went back up to Wales for a short visit and had a look at the pups to see which one we would get. The mum is very old and was 13 when she had the pups and couldn't be bothered looking after them anymore, so three weeks after the return visit, we brought Metisse home, and she was only five weeks old. That's too young to get a dog, but we have tried our best with her, and she is a good dog and just wants to play with every other dog that she sees. Her full name is Metisse, but we call her Tisse.

In Year 10, we had the English speaking exam. As I started coming into school for one morning a week, this was when I was going to do it. I wrote my speech about needing to be 18 to play some games but you can join the army at 16. On the day of the speaking exam, I was one of the last people to do it. It was all going well until I got halfway through it, and I lost where I was up to on my sheet of paper. I was trying to find where I was up to for about 10 seconds, and there was just silence. This was when I decided that I was going to restart. I told my teacher I fucked it and needed to start again. I had another go at my speech, and it wasn't perfect in the slightest but was way better than what had just happened. I wasn't bothered about my speech and how it went because I thought that I didn't need to do an exam to prove that I could speak English.

After my speaking exam, nothing really happened until the summer holidays. What annoyed me at school was having to wear a mask while I wore glasses. Every time I put a mask on my glasses would steam up.

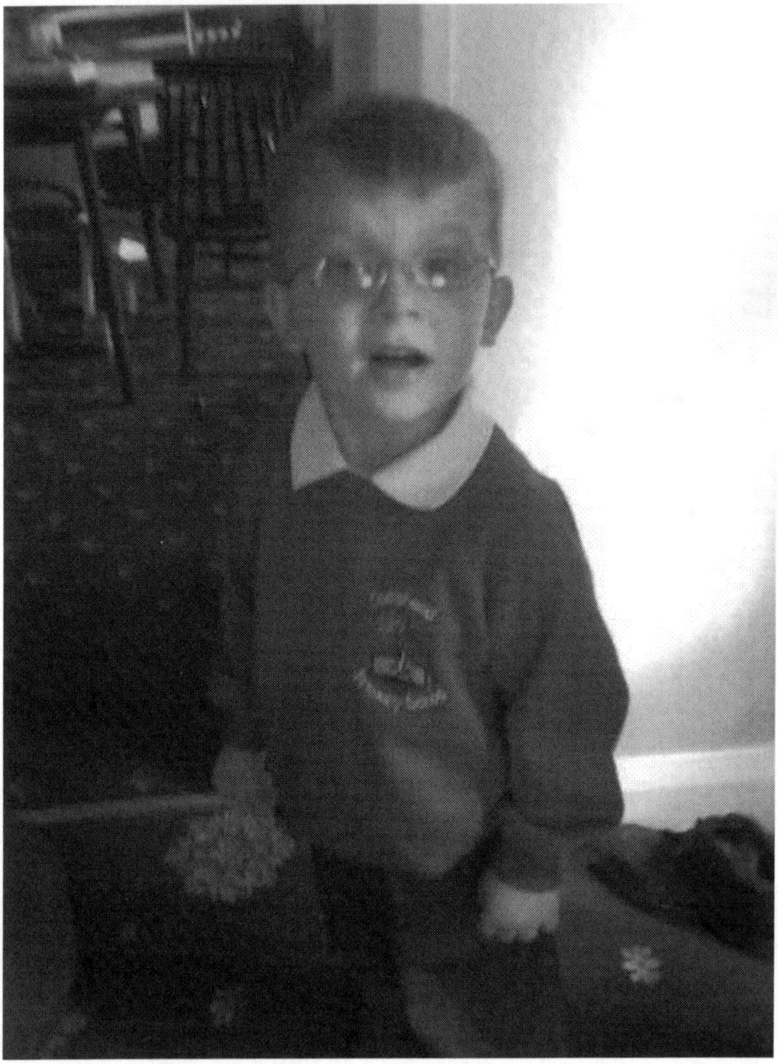

Figure 1 Ready for my first day at school.

Figure 2 Me on a race bike with my brother Fred eating a sandwich.

Figure 3 Graham teaching me how to ride the mini moto.

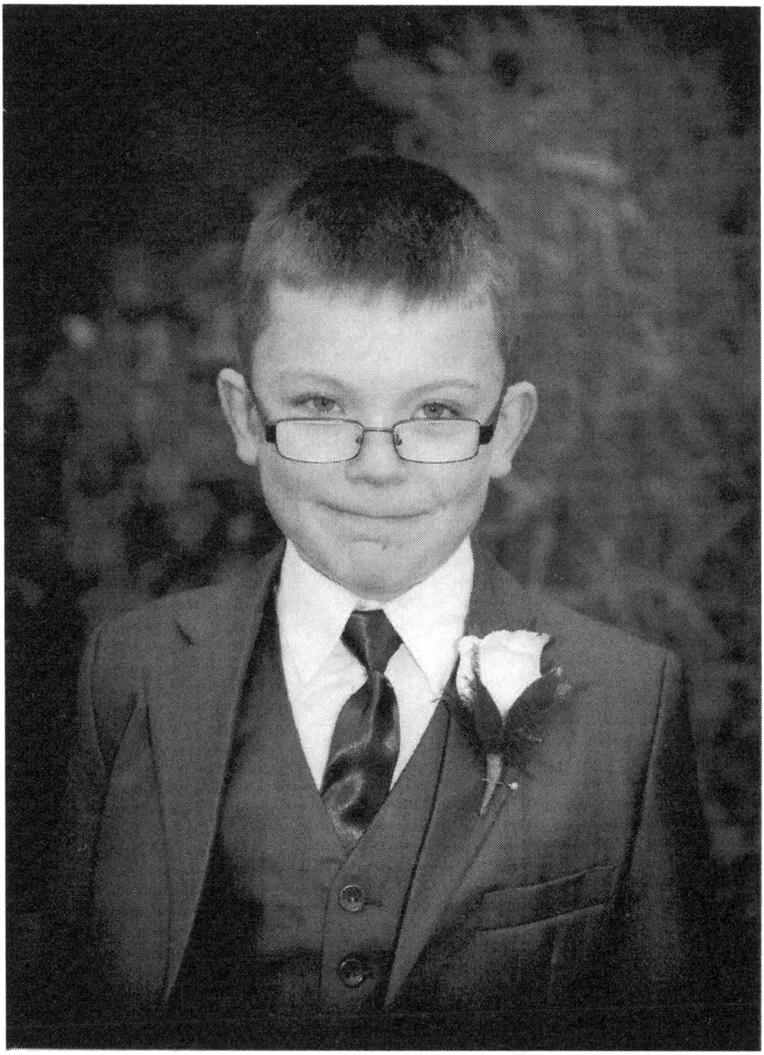

Figure 4 Me as best man at my mum's and stepdad's wedding.

Figure 5 My mum and stepdad Graham as I mention them a lot.

Figure 6 Me and my uncle Scott.

Figure 7 Me at my pass out parade at Air Cadets.

Figure 8 Me with my lockdown haircut ready to go to prom with my half brother and sister Joe and May.

Figure 9 Me and my grandad ready to set off to the NABD rally.

Figure 10 Me at the local park on my AJS.

Figure 11 Sensei Mike Lynch awarding me my red belt.

Figure 12 Me playing pool on my 18th birthday.

Sixteen to seventeen years old

The next big thing that I was looking forward to was getting on the road. For my 16th birthday, I was getting a moped and doing my test to ride it. The moped I ended up getting was a Honda SFX 50, and it was older than me. Before my birthday, I found out that I needed to fill in a form so I would be allowed to park in the school car park. I asked my head of year numerous times to send me this form, but I didn't receive it. It was getting on my nerves that he wasn't giving me this form; I think he didn't want me to turn up on my own bike. Fed up, I was going to ask him one more time for this form, and if he didn't send it, I was going to turn up on my bike anyway. The last time I asked him, he actually gave it to me; it had only taken two months.

I didn't start riding straight after my birthday, as I had to wait until I had completed my test. My Compulsory Basic Training was booked on 6th December 2020, which was a Sunday. The night before my training, I smashed a bowl and cut my knuckle open. All we did was stick some Steri-Strips on the cut and put a plaster on.

The next day, I woke up at 7am, as my training started at 8am. On the way there, it was heaving it down, and it did all day. I did the first part of the training and passed, but the problem that I had was the figure of eight; I had to use my left hand to operate the back brake to control the speed. Another problem was I had a habit of looking at the ground. I tried my best to fix my issues and passed the first section of training. One thing that I knew from the get-go was I had to stop with my left leg on the ground instead of my right leg. This is the correct way to stop when doing your bike test and doing anything different results in a fail. I didn't find it hard doing it on my left, but it was unnatural.

I then went out on the road. This section of the test is meant to last two hours, but on that day, it lasted three hours. The rain was coming down so hard it was bouncing off the ground. We had just finished the U-turn and emergency stop when my instructor told me to phone someone to pick me up, and I remember taking my glove off and the plaster and Steri-Strips peeling off my hand. I told my parents that I was going to be done soon, and then I had the task of putting my wet glove on my hand without making the cut worse.

On the way back to the test centre, I made a mistake. After a long ride in bad conditions, I misjudged how far a car was on a roundabout and entered the roundabout. It was not the safest thing that I had done. Back at the test centre, my instructor told me that I got my certificate just because I made no other mistakes, but I must be more careful on roundabouts. From then on, I have double-checked before going onto a roundabout.

I was in the car on the way home at 3.30pm. I got a phone call from an insurance company, as my mum was trying to get my insurance before all the firms shut early on Sunday. This was so I could ride to school on Tuesday. After the long day, I went to bed at 8pm. The next morning, I was so sore in my left leg because I had overused it. I went to school that day, and Graham checked my moped over to see if it would start, which it didn't.

The following week, Graham managed to get it running, and I rode it to school. For the first few days, everybody was amazed when they saw me with my wheels and kept asking, 'Is it yours?'

After a week went by, it was old news, and *almost* nobody was bothered anymore.

I say this because there was a girl and her friend who kept coming over to my group. They had been over to see what we were doing before, but at this point, they were coming over every day. These girls were annoying all of us, but they were annoying me in particular, as they were stroking my hair and pinching my ears. I found out that one of the girls was stalking my mum's Facebook page, and she had looked back through her posting history – as far back as five years. When I went home on the day, I found out she was going through my mum's Facebook, I told my mum what was happening, and she told me that this girl liked me. I had a thought that crossed my mind that she might like me, but I was not interested at all. I told the teacher that this girl was following me and my group of friends, and all the teacher did was ask her to go away. Do you reckon that worked?

It didn't work, and I was getting fed up with her doing this type of thing to me every day, so I took matters into my own hands. I took her bag off her and threw it over the fence onto the field. The teacher who got her bag didn't ask why I did it; he just belittled me and questioned what sort of person is silly enough to do such a thing. He was more bothered about getting his shoes muddy. It was only after this incident that they listened to what I had already been saying, so I was told to tell them every time this girl was being weird. For the next few days, I tried this, but she was even stroking my head in front of the teacher, and nothing was actually happening. My friends thought that this was ridiculous, so one of them helped me get her bag so I could throw it again.

This time, I emptied her bag all over the ground first, then threw it over. As I had done it again, me and my friend were made to stand next to the teacher for the rest of lunch – at least this girl couldn't annoy me. The teachers were more bothered about her books that could have been wrecked because they were on the ground than what was happening to me. I tell you what, she stopped coming over to me and stopped messing with me after I did it again and nothing the school did worked. Maybe if it was the other way round, it would have been dealt with differently.

Everyone got a lot more serious in Year 11, as they wanted to do well in their GCSEs, and I was no different. My parents had doubts about me getting my head down in the last year, but I knew I would do it. In the previous years, I'd decided that I wouldn't do the work, but I did all the work I was given in Year 11. At the start of December, there were mock tests in all subjects. It was extra important that I got good results in these tests, as they would be used if we went into another lockdown. In all honesty, I can't remember what I got in these exams, but I think that I must have done alright.

After Christmas, I started doing revision sessions at school. After I got home every night, I would go to my gran's where it was quiet and I could use her computer. She would also make me my tea. That was rinse and repeat for weeks until it was my GCSE week. The reason why I said it was good that I started my GCSEs in Year 9 was because my last year was just revision – in schools where they started in Year 10, they were still going over new material in the last year due to the lockdowns.

Outside of school, not much was happening except I was already looking for a bigger bike for when I turned 17. At 17, you are allowed up to 125cc on the same licence. I like the old-looking bikes, especially the AJS Cadwell 125. I found one for sale not too far away in Wales. We went to pick the bike up and got stuck in traffic on the motorway. When we got to the bike, it was someone selling it for their son. The bike seemed alright. Graham had a run round the streets, and there were no major problems with it, so I bought it and brought it back home. I then just had to wait before I could ride it.

The week of my GCSEs, I was cool as a cucumber going into the hall and doing my exam and doing more revision until I went home. I did that until my exams were over. As soon as the exams were over, the talk was just purely about prom. For months, people in my year were talking about prom and what they were going to wear, and I found it irritating. School told us that there was a chance we wouldn't have a prom this year and everyone went mental, so they had to put something on.

I was not going to go because I saw it as another day at school where you just talk to your friends, but all dressed up. My gran told me even if I didn't want to go, I should go anyway, as it might be good and if I wasn't there, I might regret it. It was only for that reason I went to prom.

I waited until the day of my prom and went on my moped. All

it consisted of was going to school in a suit to say bye to people and have an assembly and have some food. The girl who stalked me and would stroke my hair had left me alone after I threw her bag, but on the last day, she just followed me around trying to get a picture taken with me. As soon as the gates were open, I left; I was the first person to leave that day and just went home. The prom was just how I thought it would be, and if I knew it was going to be like that, I wouldn't have even gone.

As I hated school, I didn't want to do anything that resembled it after. That meant that going to college was off the table in my eyes. The only other option that I had was an apprenticeship. I wasn't looking for an apprenticeship; I must have been hoping that everything would be sorted for me. I did have a little look for jobs and apprenticeships, and I wanted to be a wagon driver, but you need your car licence first. Eventually, I ran out of time to apply for an apprenticeship, and the only option I had was go to college. School doesn't help you find employment after you leave, but they push for you to stay in education and go to college. I didn't put much thought into which one I went to; my uncle went to one many years ago and liked it, so that was where I went. Picking which course I would do was also simple; I did the one that sounded most like the Air Cadets that I was in. The course I ended up doing was Uniformed Protective Services.

After I finished school, I had nearly 10 weeks before I went to college. At the end of high school, people were getting jobs as waiters in pubs and in chippies. I was also encouraged by both my parents and grandparents to get a job. This was when I considered the difficulties of being a waiter. There was no way I could be a waiter with one hand that could not hold a plate or barely pick a glass up. I considered it because if I wanted to be a waiter, there were a few jobs that I could apply for. I looked for jobs, but none of them were anything I wanted to do in the slightest, and the ones that I did apply for did not get back to me, so I stopped looking for a job. There was always a job that I could get, and that was being a pot washer where my uncle used to work. He even said that he would put in a word for me. The reason I didn't do this job was because he said it was hard work and that I would struggle. I thought to myself that if he struggled to do the job, then there was not much chance of me being able to do it. I stayed jobless for the rest of my holidays.

My mum wanted to get out of the house for her 40th birthday, so my present to her was looking after my siblings and dogs while she went to Whitby. I looked after everyone and kept them occupied by taking them to the park and such. My gran was there to help if anything went wrong, but she also offered to make us all our tea, which would be stupid for me to turn down. Joe and May enjoyed me looking after them, as I would allow them to get away with a little more than they could otherwise. All was well except one problem that really wasn't a problem in the end. My dog, Tisse, was stressed as we all went to my gran's for tea, and she ripped all the carpet up upstairs. This didn't matter because we were getting a new carpet put down after my parents came back anyway. If anything, Tisse had done half of the carpet fitters' job getting the old stuff up off the floor.

The first taster of the college that I go to now was an open day. I didn't know where my college was to begin with, but Graham went on his bike and I went on mine while he showed me the way, like big duck and little duck. On the way there, I tried to overtake a tractor on the dual carriageway on my moped and did not succeed. That was possibly not my brightest idea, but that is what I did. When I got there, Graham went home. The open day showed me around the college and around the zoo that they have there. It was actually the head of my department who showed me round that day. It was outlandishly hot, and I kept my bike jacket on – I was being cooked alive. The open day wasn't great to be honest, but at least I knew where the college was after going there. As Graham had left, I had to find my own way back, which I found no problem.

While I was off, I went to the Hells Angels clubhouse for a night out. My grandad, Phil Carpenter, is popular in the area for what he did in his racing career and for who he is as a person. Over the years, he has got to know the Hells Angels and likes to go to the night that they have on. This particular time, I was brought along, and it was busy. I sat on the couch and relaxed while watching the band that was on until we decided to head home when it was fairly late on in the night. I found out that some of the Hells Angels noticed my walking and thought that I was getting too drunk. I wasn't that bad; my left leg made me look worse than I was. It doesn't help that my walking gets worse when I have a drink.

Before I knew it, results day came, and I went back to school to pick them up. Everyone was there saying hi to each other, as they hadn't seen each other since prom. I got my results and checked if I had got anything less than a four (pass), which I didn't, so I wasn't bothered. I then got my leavers' hoodie and went home. Even though I checked my results, I didn't know what exactly I got. My parents wanted to know what I got, so they had a look, and it turned out that I did quite well. The lowest I got was a five, and the highest I got was an eight. I don't get why people were getting money of their parents as a reward for passing their GCSEs. They should have wanted to do their best anyway after spending 12 years in school.

I got what I needed to go on the level three Uniformed Protective Services course at college. I just needed to show them my results.

Two days after getting my GCSE results, I had to bring them into college to see whether I qualified to be on the course that I had picked. On the way there, I took the wrong turn and went all round the streets nearby before I got to the college. As I pulled up, there was a group of people who went into the sports hall where we would be processed ready for our first day. I waited 30 minutes before anyone spoke to me; then I gave my results to them, and they put me down for the level three course. After that, they took my picture and gave me my lanyard. The next time that I went to college was my first day.

I had a referral from the children's hospital to go and see the occupational therapists. When I went to my appointment, they gave me stretches and also said that going to the gym would help me greatly. We then discussed where the best place for me to get help from was. At this appointment, I was with the children's occupational therapist even though I was 16; they said that they would struggle to get me into the adults' occupational therapy because I was not 18. They did try to get me in with the other adults, but because of my age, I was in no man's land.

With my time off from school/college, I was beginning to get bored, and as it was recommended to me, I joined the gym. I was new to the gym and wanted help and guidance, so I got a personal trainer to help me get started. He wasn't from the area and had to travel to my gym, and that was part of the reason that he was expensive. He gave me a tailored programme that would help both sides equal out. Each session that I did I was trying my best. I was even doing my best to eat healthily with a lot of protein. It was all going well for me; I was making progress doing the rehabilitation exercises that I was given. There was just one problem: I wasn't doing the stretches that I was given.

I had another appointment with the occupational therapists, and just by walking into the room, they already knew that I had started going to the gym and wasn't doing the stretches I was told to. I was then given more stretches; these were to help my back and aid in walking better. Guess what? I didn't do these either, and I will tell you why. Firstly, doing stretches every day is just boring to me, and I would have to force myself to do them every time. The second reason that ties in with the first reason is that doing them was a reminder that my arm and leg don't work as they are supposed to.

I stupidly stopped going to the gym, as I wasn't seeing the progress I wanted and started to struggle doing some exercises. The impeding factor was my grip strength; I would lose my grip before the other muscles would receive the benefit of the exercise. I should have carried on, and eventually, I would have been able to pull the weight needed.

My first day of college, I rode up on my moped and was walking all around the college until I found the class that I was in. While trying to find my class, I had to phone my mum to tell her that I was okay and had made it to college. In class, there were 24 of us. We were given our timetables and were only in three days a week: I had Thursday, Friday, Saturday and Sunday off. We then all did two truths and a lie to get to know a little bit about each other. Not much else happened that day except going to class and starting an assignment already. I didn't know where the toilets were, so I asked a teacher, and she showed me the way to the girls' bathroom, for a reason unknown to myself.

After a few days, I started to figure out who I liked and what people were all about. I was very opinionated towards some people from the beginning. Throughout the year, some people changed my opinion of them, and others just made my opinion even stronger.

At the same time as starting college, my family received bad news about my mum. Over the past few years, my mum has suffered with migraines. This has caused her to be in bed for weeks at a time. She has also complained of being tired all the time and needs to sleep throughout the day. All of our family thought that my mum was just making excuses to get back in bed for an extra hour of sleep. One day, my mum was bedbound from stomach ache. It was so bad that Graham took her to the hospital. The hospital took my mum's blood, thinking that it would confirm gallstones. The hospital said she mustn't go home until she had spoken to a doctor. My mum was trying to get out of the hospital because my sister was having a lot of teeth pulled out the next day. They explained that she needed a specialist appointment urgently, as the blood results were very worrying; the results were pointing to leukaemia. My mum just had to ride the pain until it went away. The doctors did tell my mum not to Google what it could be so as not to scare herself. They found that her potassium levels were high, just like when she had sepsis. This led to her trying to find ways to lower potassium without scaring herself. The solution that she had was eating only white bread with cauliflower for the majority of the time until her next blood appointment.

At this specialist appointment, my mum was diagnosed with a blood condition that is classed as a form of cancer but is not deadly.

This means that she has the symptoms associated with leukaemia but with a more positive outcome. This explains why she was and is always tired. To add insult to injury, she has also been diagnosed with chronic fatigue syndrome, which can be caused by having severe sepsis.

While we were waiting for the next appointment, I wasn't worried, and I can only think of two reasons why. The first reason was that my mum didn't talk about it much so she didn't put her worries on other people. The second reason might be that I wanted to ignore what was happening.

As I was 16 and not a child anymore, I would no longer go to the children's hospital, but I went one last time. The appointment was at 1pm, and I went to college that morning. Graham went on his bike to my college. He rode in front of me, and I was following him through the middle of Manchester. I didn't have a clue where I was going, as everywhere looked the same to me. We both made it to the hospital and had to wait to be seen. When I was called to go and see my doctor, the nurse was surprised when I came walking through holding my helmet. I wasn't even going to add this in the book until Graham said it was funny so I should.

When I sat down, the first thing that the doctor asked was whether I had come on my own bike. All I said was yes. They then asked again to double-check, and I said yes again. The doctor was shocked that I had got to the hospital on two wheels. The doctor then asked if I rode through the middle of Manchester, and I bet you can't guess what I said next. As they were trying to fathom how I rode to the hospital, I was thinking to myself, *It doesn't really count, as I followed Graham to get here*. Graham told me that it is easy to follow someone and a lot harder to do it yourself; that is why I didn't count it in my head. Graham also said the appointment was like pulling teeth because of my one-word answers. He also told me the doctors looked shocked, surprised and a little bit horrified, I'm guessing because I rode to the appointment. They then moved on to the functionality of my hand, and they weren't bothered because I had managed to ride to the hospital. If I was able to do that, then I must be able to get on with life without much struggle. I was then signed off, and that was the last time that I went to the children's hospital.

The next thing that happened was my grandad inviting me down to the pool night. We were away at another pub, but it wasn't too far away. The only person that I knew there was my grandad, and I'd never met the other people on the team before. I had been to this pub before – watching my uncle play in a tournament – and it is a good setup. I watched my grandad's game. Other people, while waiting for their game of pool, were playing snooker. As stupid as it sounds, I didn't want to have a shot on the snooker table because I used a different guide to everyone else. I was asked if I wanted a shot, but I didn't, so I said no. They weren't going to take no for an answer and gave me their cue. I even tried to give the cue back and said that I was terrible at pool.

I took a shot, and the red travelled the distance of the table and went in the pocket. If you don't know much about pool or snooker, that is incredibly hard to do when you don't play. Everyone who saw me do that said that I must be good if I could do that, and I told them that it was beginner's luck because it was. All the games were played, and I remember thinking that the team is good so we must have won the night. On the way home, me and my grandad called in at our local pub. After that, I went home. I liked going to watch the pool on a Tuesday with my grandad, so I went every week. I had a game of pool where I could, so one day, I may have been good enough to join the team.

My grandad, from being my age, has been going to bike rallies. There was one coming up, and he invited me to tag along with his friends. It was only a few miles down the road and was a perfect little run for me on my moped. Luckily, the weather held off that weekend, and the ride there was pleasant but slow. The field that we were camping on was at a farm, which had donkeys and alpacas. We then pitched our tents and cracked a can. I quickly realised that I was going to be pampered and looked after when I was getting food made for me and was being asked whether I was okay often. The band was at the horse paddock, and it was full of foam. Later that night, the band was on, and there was a woman dancing by herself. My grandad's friends were all saying go up and dance with her, and there was no way that I was going to do that.

The next day, we got up at 7am, and I had breakfast made for me. We were then chilling until dinnertime, when we had a look round at the stalls that were there. This was where I bought my leather cut (waistcoat), as I didn't have one but wanted one. I looked at all the bikes that were there and listened to more music at night. My grandad was speaking to some people that he met and was talking about him winning the senior TT in 1974. It was at that point I realised how well known my grandad was and how many people wanted to know his story. Later that day, there was a person teasing me, but he soon stopped when he realised the old man standing next to me was Phil Carpenter and he was my grandad. That showed me the respect that my grandad has from other people just for being himself. We then went and watched the band for the last time. We didn't stay at the marquee long, as we had an early night so we could leave and get home in good time the next day.

I was woken up by everybody speaking outside, and it was 6.30am. I don't know how I got up at that time. We then just drank brews before it was a reasonable time to pack up and get ready to leave. Me and my grandad were ready to leave but were waiting for the rest of our group to get their tent down. My grandad said that Decca and Terry were like husband and wife, fighting over the best way to pack the tent up. That was the best way to put it. We were finally on the road, and it felt like it took twice as long to get back as it did to get there. That rally was the perfect first rally to ride to and have the proper experience without brothers or sisters interfering.

On 19th October 2021, I was riding to college and was going down a 50mph road on my moped when it suddenly lost power, so I pulled up at a truck stop. I was trying to start it again before I decided to phone Graham to tell him what happened. He said that he would borrow a van to pick me up. As I put the phone down, some workmen came to me after getting their breakfast and offered to take me and my moped home. I then had to phone Graham to tell him that some kind strangers had offered to help me. I got my moped in the back of the van, and they both brought me home. The moped has been left in the back garden rotting since that day. I then had to go to college on the bus for the next three weeks before it was my birthday and I could get on my AJS. I hated being on the bus, as it took me just under an hour to get to college, whereas on my moped, it would take 20 minutes.

Seventeen to eighteen years old

My 17th birthday was on a Wednesday, and the last day that I was in college was a Wednesday. On my 17th birthday, I got myself a present, and that was my AJS. I could now ride it, but I didn't want to ride it to college on my first day. Before I went to college, I went down a couple of backstreets. This was to get a feel for the bike first before I did new speeds I had not done on a geared bike. After taking the bike down the backstreets, Graham told me that I needed to go and fill it up. Being really careful, I made my way down the road, and I guess my bike ran out of fuel 200 metres from the petrol station and I had to push it the remaining distance.

I then went on the bus to college that day, and when I walked into class, they were singing 'Happy birthday'. I was asked where my helmet was, and I told them that I would be on my bike next week. While I was off, I was doing little trips to the shop here and there to get used to my bike. After some time, I felt half-comfortable riding it.

The next Monday, I rode to and from college. When I got there, I had to phone my mum to tell her that I was okay because she was worrying about me, so I did. I remembered to do it that first time, then I forgot to phone her and she would ring reception to see if I was there, but I always told her not to worry because I would phone her if I fell off.

I kept to my promise the day after. On my way to college on my new bike, I fell off and broke my wrist. The road was damp and slippery, and I was coming up to a set of lights that went from green to amber. I immediately panicked and braked; the front slipped away, and I fell on my wrist and bonked my head. After that happened, my visor fogged up, but I could hear people. One of them put my bike on the pavement and gave me my broken clutch lever. A woman said that she would phone me an ambulance and then wandered off. The situation was a joke as there was a police car two cars behind me and an ambulance pulling out of a junction not too far away. Neither of them stopped to help me.

I phoned my mum, and there was no answer. I phoned Graham and there was no answer, so I phoned my mum again and she picked up. I told her that I had fallen off and I was okay but thought I had broken my wrist. While I was waiting for my parents to come, the shop near where I had fallen off was taking a delivery, and they said that I could keep my bike there until I could get it home. Graham managed to get my bike home, and my mum took me to hospital. I had an X-ray that confirmed my wrist was broken; they then gave me a splint to wear for the next eight weeks. After taking two paracetamol I decided to go to college.

This, was when people showed their true colours towards me. There were people asking whether I was okay or if I needed help, and there were other people who told me to my face, 'It would have been funny if I got skittled by a bus'. I will admit my arm was aching on the bus on the way home.

One of the attractions about the course when I applied to college was going to Poland to visit the Auschwitz concentration camps. To go to Poland, you needed to have your Covid vaccinations. That meant that I wasn't allowed to go, but I wasn't too bothered at the end of the day. Everyone in my class wanted to go. By the sounds of it, they weren't really interested in why they were going to Poland in the first place, but they wanted time wandering round Kraków. As travel restrictions changed frequently, the trip to Poland was delayed until the following year.

Before Christmas, we were doing a physical unit as part of my college course. The basis of this was taking some baseline results, creating an exercise programme and retaking the tests to compare results. Out of all the baseline results that we did, I was disappointed with my beep test and the 1.5-mile run. In the beep test, I got to 5.4, but my teacher did not want me to push myself too far because she was scared that I could hurt my left side. I guess I could have got to a 6 if I had pushed myself. I didn't even run but rather walked the 1.5 miles because I thought it would have done more harm than good. We would start the exercise programme after Christmas.

Days before we left college, there was a teacher trying to get people to sign up to do the bronze Duke of Edinburgh Award. After trying to do the award with the cadets and not having much luck there, I decided to try again here. We would start the award after Christmas in the New Year.

My New Year's resolution was to start running and to go from nothing to being able to do 5k. This was because I needed to improve my fitness for my tests, and I could also use it as the physical section for my Duke of Edinburgh Award. On 1st January, I downloaded an app on my phone and followed along with what it said and went out later that day. I would then try to get out three times a week until I was finished.

In the New Year, I also thought of playing the trumpet again to pass my skill section on the Duke of Edinburgh Award. I wasn't with the cadets anymore, so I decided that I would try and play in the local band. I went down to the band and sat through a session, and they gave me a number for a tutor for lessons. For the Duke of Edinburgh Award, you also need to do volunteering. I decided that I was going to walk a dog for someone who couldn't do it themselves anymore.

At the start of 2022, enough time had passed for my wrist to heal, and I could start driving lessons. It took my mum seven goes to pass her test, and we went through all the driving teachers in the area; my mum said that if I didn't like the driving teacher I got, I should try another one. I had a lesson with my first driving teacher, and I thought they were alright. I had another lesson booked in two weeks' time and had to wait until then. The first lesson, I didn't even drive but got used to the clutch and where the gears were. Graham was shocked that I didn't even drive the car.

Around the same time, college had some speakers from the local council who were looking for people my age to help in a youth leisure service. These speakers were talking about the opportunities that came with the job if you were into sports, but that wasn't what interested me. They were saying that they operated all over Salford so people who had their own transport would be more suitable for them, as transport meant you could go to any job. It paid £9.50 an hour, which was really good at my age.

The minimum wage was £4.62 an hour. They also said that at the start, you would be volunteering. I then got my form tutor to send me the application form to fill in. As this was the first official job that I would have, I needed to create a CV.

I then handed in my application online, and a few days later, I had an interview online through a video call. They were asking me questions like what I would do if a child was not listening. The interview was successful, and I was in contact with the boss and was told to go to a school far from where I lived. Of course, it wasn't a problem, but a few days before I went to the school, I went to the area so I could get there on time on my first day.

On the day, I got there and was quickly shown round the school. Then, I sat with the children and did arts and crafts with them. This was when I found out that it was essentially babysitting. There was a big problem that day, which was that one of the kids got McDonald's delivered to the school. The staff didn't understand how the food had got into the school. I went home, and later that day, I got sent a form asking where I lived and when I was available. I filled the form in, and the only day that I got was a Friday night – going to the youth club that I used to go to.

I think that they gave me this day as it was the session nearby, but that did not matter because I had my own bike to get to different places. I would turn up on a Friday to volunteer my time, and there would be four staff plus myself for a club that only had a few kids in. I think the most that we had was five kids one night. Some nights, we had no kids turn up, so there was literally nothing to do. I got to know the people I was with, and I knew one of them already because she used to look after me when I was small. When I used to go to the youth club, it was full, but they had changed the building since.

There was then a training day coming up that was held in the sports hall of my college. The night before the training day, I got a phone call from my boss saying that I was not what they were looking for, so I didn't need to turn up anymore. He then said that they could set up a video call to go over what I needed to do to be better for next time. That is because he said I was more than welcome to apply again when they were recruiting. I didn't think that was fair really because I was attending a session where I was not able to show my capability to do the job that they needed done because there were no kids turning up. I didn't want a meeting over what I could have done better, as I thought that it was just a way of them saying that they didn't need another person on the session on a Friday night. Looking back, I should have done it regardless, but I didn't. If it was a Friday night that was a problem, I could have travelled.

What they did next, which I thought was stupid, was probably around a month later from the phone call. They were advertising for the job again at college. My teacher asked how it was going at the job. When she found out that I had got sacked from volunteering, she was more than willing to write an email to them to tell them about the mistake that they had made. This is because I was better than other people she knew who had got a job there. I didn't want her to send an email because I didn't want to deal with them anymore. They weren't even paying me for attending the Friday nights and still sacked me but were looking for new people. They could have just given me the training the day after the phone call, kept me on and allowed me to progress to a standard that they wanted.

While I was trying to get a job in the youth leisure service, a girl on my course at college who also worked for the leisure service was trying to get my attention. She was called Poppy. One day, she just randomly came over to me, gave me a hug and called me her best friend. In general, she was a very lively person and would do random things all the time. It confused me as to why she did it, but knowing what she was like, I shrugged it off and didn't think any more of it. Over time, Poppy started to flirt with me more and more, but it was like water off a duck's back – I didn't have a clue. After a month of her flirting, I did stop and think she may be flirting with me, but I wasn't sure. I was only certain when her friend Caitlin told me that Poppy liked me. Knowing what she was like and what she got up to in her own time, I was in a position to decide what I was going to do next. I decided that it would be more effort than it was worth to have her as my girlfriend. Shortly after,

Poppy stopped flirting with me as much.

At college, there was a person who started going to Brazilian jiu-jitsu, and he didn't stop talking about how good it was. He talked about the tournaments he was entering as a white belt. I looked into jiu-jitsu – like I had when I was younger – and I had the same luck. I still wanted to do martial arts but didn't know where to go. There were posters on the wall of my local pub for the karate dojo that is next door. I completely forgot about the dojo next to the pub until I came home from playing pool; I told my gran that I wanted to do martial arts, and she told me I needed to ask someone in the local pub about joining.

The next Tuesday, I did just that. Me and the pool team were away and a player short, so the captain tried to sign me on. As the team sheet was full, I couldn't be signed on – the players couldn't be changed once they had signed on. It was at that point I knew it would be next season before I got to play for the team. After watching the team play pool at the other team's pub, me and my grandad headed towards our local pub, and I told the person who already went to karate that I was interested in joining. He said that he would pass my interest on to the person in charge.

I waited a few weeks and asked what the person in charge had said. The person who I had shown my interest to said that I would have to wait a few more weeks before I could join but that I could come down next Monday to look at what they did. That's exactly what I did. I went to the dojo, and I watched two people sparring.

One of the sensei asked me a question. 'Why do you want to do karate?'

I told him about my arm and leg not working properly and that I have poor coordination. He then said that I had come to the right place, as in karate, you need to be just as strong on one side as you are on the other.

The first session that I did at the dojo was on 14th February 2022. What else do you do on Valentine's Day? The sensei just took me over the basics of punching and how to move forwards and backwards. I kept coming every Monday. I slowly built upon my punches and progressed to blocks, and from forwards and backwards to side movements. This meant that I could start my first kata. A kata is a sequence of moves to be practised in good form – a routine, if you like.

At first, my sensei wanted me to notice the movement pattern of the kata, as it looked like the letter H on its side. We ran through that multiple times and then involved our hands with our legs at the same time, and I struggled. My sensei told me everyone finds it difficult the first time they do this; I found it especially hard because of my poor coordination. It took me many, many weeks to do it to a reasonable standard.

A problem that we faced was that the tendons in my left hand were tight – when I try to form a fist, my middle knuckle on my first finger sticks out. This is bad because when you strike, you can hurt your hand easily. This is a challenge that I still face today, but I am closer now than I was back then to being able to use my left hand as a weapon. The way that we have tried to get my hand to work is through experimentation. This means that I would not be as good as someone else with karate experience on the street, so my sensei has taught a fighting style best for me. After I reached a good standard in the first kata, I moved on to learn the cat stance. This was to be used in the second kata. I have found this really difficult to do because the front foot has the heel raised. This has been hard for me with my left leg, but after much repetition, I am able to do it sufficiently.

My driving was slowly getting better but could have been better faster. I had eight lessons, and I wasn't even off the backstreets. Eventually, I got to go out on the main road and only did one lesson; then I didn't have a lesson for a while because my driving teacher was moving house for six weeks. The next lesson that I had was on the backstreets again.

Caitlin turned 18 and had a birthday party that was further away than college, so the only way to get there was on my motorbike. I am not really the type of person that likes to go to parties – I like to go to the pub instead – but I did go to this one. In the area where the party was, there are two pubs with similar names. I typed the name of the right pub into Google, and it gave me the postcode of the other pub. I ended up getting to the pub, and I asked at the bar if there was a party going on there because I saw no one else from my class. People in the pub were saying that there was a party, so I waited for the other people to turn up outside. Eventually, I decided to go inside, and to my surprise, it was a man's 50th birthday – not Caitlin's 18th birthday. This was when I phoned up my friend, and we figured out I had gone to the wrong pub. I then got back on my bike, went a mile and a half down the road and got to the right pub. This was the first party that I had ever gone to, and I enjoyed it. There were only six of us from college – it was not just me who did not like people in our class. All six of us did not like the same people. hat was why it was just us six at the party from our college.

One of the other five people there I knew from my first primary school, and the last time I spoke to her was seven years previously. She was the one involved in why I didn't see my dad in seven years, it was the person I told why I thought my stepbrother moved to my school. I was speaking to my friends all night, but I was not fully there, as I was thinking about my dad in the back of my mind. It was the first time that I had properly thought about him since I stopped seeing him.

As Poppy was best friends with Caitlin, she was there, and she was trying her best to get me to dance with her. I am not a party animal who likes to dance, do karaoke and drink themselves senseless. I didn't want to dance with her, and my sober mind was busy thinking about what had happened all that time ago. I think it was her last-ditch effort to have me, but I already made my mind up about her. My decision wasn't going to change just because I was at a party.

My friend came up with the idea to take a picture of us all and send it to our form tutor. The night was drawing to a close, so I handed a card to Caitlin saying thank you for the invite. People then wanted me to let them know that I got home safe, so they put their numbers in my phone so I could message them when I got back, which I did. The next time that we went into college, my form tutor was showing us the photo that we sent to her and said that she laughed when she got it.

It was soon after the party that we redid the physical tests before Christmas for our baselines. From the New Year, I kept running regularly, but as the sessions started to get longer, I was finding myself getting bored. I thought that I would carry on to pass my Duke of Edinburgh Award. At the end of the physical unit, I managed to run 5k on the treadmill in around 33 minutes. I also retook the beep test and scored significantly higher than before. I managed to get a score of 9.8, and I physically couldn't go any quicker. My teacher was not worried about me pushing myself this time, as she knew that I had been training.

I did the 5k on the treadmill at college, but I didn't stretch beforehand. This led to me getting an injury that lasted three weeks, so I couldn't carry on running after I completed my goal for my Duke of Edinburgh. I noticed that the longer runs were making my left leg tight, and it got to point that it hindered my karate. That was even when doing 10 minutes of stretching before and after every single run, except that one 5k I did. With my injury and the running affecting me at karate as well as it being boring for me, I decided to stop running altogether.

Next, I went to the NABD rally as well as a sidecar rally in Birmingham, just weeks apart from each other. The war between Russia and Ukraine meant that the trip to Poland was cancelled. This didn't bother me, as I was not going to go in the first place because I didn't have my Covid vaccination, but I did have the rallies to look forward to.

The first rally of the year was the NABD. As mentioned, this was not my first time at this rally; it was my grandad's first time, though. It is only down the road for us. I left my airbed and sleeping bag at the caravan in Anglesey, so I needed to get another sleeping bag and airbed. One week before the rally, I ordered a sleeping bag and airbed. The sleeping bag came, but the airbed did not. It actually came three hours after I left to go to the rally.

My bike was out of commission because I didn't look after it properly and forgot to put oil in it. What can I say? I just like riding bikes and forget to look after them. Luckily, Graham knows what he is doing and keeps my bike together. This would have been a perfect little run for my bike, but unfortunately, I couldn't ride to the rally and had to get a lift instead. After not being able to get there myself, I started checking the oil in my bike regularly. Decca had turned a Reliant Robin into a trike, so I got to the rally in the back of that. On the way there, we stopped off at a pub to wait for Terry to meet up with us from Birmingham. As we pulled up, we realised that all my grandad's gear was hanging off the side of his bike. After rearranging the gear on the back of his bike, my grandad realised that he had lost his bog roll. We got to the site early so we could pick where we pitched our camp.

After setting the camp up, we started drinking our beers. We chilled out and watched the field fill up with tents. Then, we had a look around. Terry got me my first rally hat. It was a fez. I wore that hat the entire weekend. Everybody was asking about it. I was asked where I got it and was told that I looked like the comedian Tommy Cooper. We then went back to camp, and everyone except me and Jarvo, another member of the rally group, went to sleep before the music started. The weather then turned that night, and it started to rain.

The best place to go was the beer tent, where you could listen to the band and get a few pints down. People liked my hat so much that they wanted to have pictures with me. I was listening to the band when a lady asked my grandad to go and dance with her. He did not want to, and as I was next to him, I was dragged to the front and started to dance. I did not have a clue what I was doing, but I went with the flow. We then called it a night and went back to camp and to bed.

It was not the most comfortable night's sleep I'd ever had, as I was on the cold hard floor, but it didn't bother me too much. The people I was sharing the tent with said that they had to step over me to get out of the tent to go to the toilet.

The next morning, I woke up at 7.30am and had one cup of tea before I had a shot of Jägermeister. It wasn't even 8am, and I was drinking. The rain blew over, and the sun was out all day. We then ate breakfast. We put sausage and egg on the BBQ. I then felt sick when everyone else was buttering their barms. A little later, I got a message from my friend from college saying that he would come down for a few hours and have a look round. He came later than he said because he couldn't find the site. He was confused when he saw me walk up with my fez on.

We then had a look at the bikes and trikes that were on show. With all the walking around that I was doing in bike boots, my feet were getting sore, and I was struggling to walk. My friend then left shortly after to go to another show. Terry bought me a roll mat so that I wouldn't sleep in front of the door. I then went looking in the beer tents for the crew. Sure enough, they were in there. We had a few pints before we had to go back for a rest and a bite to eat. Me and my grandad then wandered off to go and listen to the music. I remember going to the bar because I wanted a Coke. The only non-alcoholic drink I had over those two days was a cup of tea in the morning. What can I say, the rally group made from mostly old, aged pensioners is a bad influence on me.

We then sat outside drinking. I noticed that people weren't that interested in my fez anymore. That was because many people were wearing them on the second day. The rally hat that I started wearing became a trend.

At the end of the night, there were strippers. I went into the tent to see what it was like. The tent was full, and everybody in there was pushing and shoving to get to the front for a better view; they were like animals. I was then getting cans thrown at my head. It was more effort than it was worth, so I just went back to camp before the strippers even came out.

I then woke up early and didn't feel the best. I think it was a mix of dehydration and sunstroke, so I thought the best thing was to finish off a bottle of Glayva so we would not have to take it home. All but one of us packed our gear away. It took a lot longer than it should have to get packed up and on the road. We then got home, and my gran made me some toasties before she dropped me off at my house.

Next was the sidecar rally in Birmingham. It was an experience. Me, my grandad and Decca set off at 9.15am. Overall, I enjoyed the ride, especially the first leg of the journey. As I was on a 125cc, I was not allowed on the motorway, so I had to get to Aston Stanlow on A-roads from the outskirts of Salford. I overtook my first vehicle on the road; it was a tractor that we were stuck behind. At the start of the ride, there were many bendy roads, which were satisfying to go down. Then, we got onto the A-road that took us straight to Birmingham city centre. We were only doing 30–40 mph, so it took longer to make progress. This was because of the fully loaded Reliant Robin trike. We pulled over to go to the toilet and have a drink. I was thankful for the five minutes of rest because my left wrist was aching from the pressure on the bars, which aggravated my previously broken wrist.

After a quick pit stop, we headed for Terry's house, going through Birmingham. His wife made us a brew before we did the last leg of the journey. The last few miles were down country lanes, and it seemed as though we'd entered a maze. If we wanted to get back to Birmingham, we needed Terry to show us the way. We were on the road for six hours that day. After such a long ride, we cracked a can while setting up camp. We struggled to set up camp because of the intense heat. All four of us shared a big tent that we slept in, and we set up an outside area. I had my airbed with me this time.

There were chickens that were wandering around, and one fell asleep under my chair. My grandad was feeding his crusts to the chickens. After tea, we went to the local pub. That weekend, we were drinking Guinness, and I got the taste for it. After many pints (and some whisky later), I stumbled back to the tent, which is easier said than done with a leg that doesn't work properly. To get back to the site from the pub, you had to walk through a graveyard. We then had some Glayva to finish off the night before we went to sleep.

The next morning, it was overcast, and there were intermittent showers. There was a ride out that day around the local area, and you would get lunch at the end. We did not join the others on the ride because we'd had a big ride the day before and it was also raining. With the others on the ride out, it left the site empty and quiet. Me, my grandad, Decca and Terry were so tired that we all fell asleep. I was woken up when a Red Arrow went over my head. I then found Decca putting things on Terry, who was still asleep and was taking pictures. The weather report said that it was going to throw it down the next day. After we had our siesta, we headed out to another pub, as there was nothing better to do. Before we went, my grandad started feeding his lunch to the chickens, and they were his best friends from then on. It reminded him of when he was on a farm.

We spent three hours at the pub, and they were all talking about what they did when they were young. I sat there listening because there was nothing that I could say that was relevant. Every time that I went to the toilet, I was finding it harder to walk back to them. Back at camp, we had our tea.

As the weather was going to be terrible the next day, people were packing up and leaving on the Saturday instead of the Sunday. We went back to the pub that we were in the night before. On the way there, we were looking round the graveyard and inside the church. I was wearing my fez, and people were asking if I liked Tommy Cooper. It was really busy in the pub that night and we had already been out that day, so we only had a couple and went back. We got back to the tent just in time because it started to rain.

I went to sleep to the sound of the rain bouncing off the tent and woke up in a puddle. The rain had poured down the entire night. We then packed the gear away inside our tent and drank brews while we were waiting for the weather to break. The rain stopped for an hour, so that was enough time to put the tent away and get packed up. We were all ready to go. My grandad was having problems trying to fire his bike up. After 20 minutes of wrestling with his bike, it started. I then went back to my bike, and that was also playing up. With a little persuasion, that fired up, too, and then we were off.

We got back to Terry's house and had a brew with the weather holding off. The heavens then opened up. We stopped off at a petrol station to fill up to be on the safe side. I also needed to go to the toilet after having a cup of tea, but there were no toilets. We were then on a long, straight road home, and the ride started to get harder. My visor fogged up and I couldn't see, so I opened it, and the rain hitting my face felt like pins and needles. My glasses then fogged up as well, so I had to look over them. I had to endure my face stinging and low visibility for the rest of the way home. There was a grid in the middle of a narrow road, and I went over it and felt the front slip. That was a little scary, but all I did was laugh it off.

Two hours later, I still needed to go to the toilet and thought that if I did piss myself, it wouldn't make a difference because I was wet through. After riding in the rain for the last three hours, we were five miles from home, so sod's law had it that the weather cleared up. As I went up my gran's drive, I jumped off my bike and relieved myself in the garden with my helmet, gloves and waterproofs still on. My mum was at Gran's house waiting for me to come home. After I finished my business, I could finally say hello to everyone now that I was able to think straight. I took my helmet off, and there were puddles of water coming out of my ears. My grandad then said if I could ride that distance on those types of roads in those sorts of conditions, I could ride anywhere. It meant a lot to me that he said that. When I got home, I had a shower to get clean and warm. This was my first big ride out.

In the first year of my course, there was just one exam that I needed to pass; otherwise, I would fail the course. I didn't want to waste the time I had spent at college, so I was making sure that I was doing all the work that I could. During this period, it was uneventful except for one thing that someone did that pushed my buttons. There was this one person in my class who just did as he pleased. The one day I didn't put the alarmed lock on my bike was the one day he decided to sit on it and get someone else to take a picture of him. If I knew about it and he'd asked beforehand, I would not have been bothered in the slightest, but that didn't happen. He thought he was entitled to sit on my bike without me knowing. He then got a picture taken pretending that my bike was his. He then had the audacity to show me that picture of him. All I did was look at it for a few seconds and walk off without saying a word to him.

The day of the exam, me and my other friends all thought that the exam was not too hard. The questions were straightforward and were on topics that we went over and over and over again. I knew coming out of the hall that I had got a high mark and forgot all about the exam because it became history. I wasn't nervous one bit for that exam, but every person that I spoke to seemed a little worried.

The weekend after the exam was the time that I did the Duke of Edinburgh expedition with college. I had completed my volunteering section and my physical section of the award and was coming to the end of the skills section (which was playing the trumpet). I packed my 70-litre Bergen that I had got while I was at cadets. I had everything I needed in my bag. I was dropped off at college and met the other people that I was doing it with. I found out that I was walking round a water park, which is a reservoir where people do water sports. The people that I was with didn't want to carry all of their gear and managed to carry the bare minimum they needed to pass the expedition; all their gear fitted into a day bag. I was the only one who was carrying all their own kit. My bag was heavy, and about halfway round this water park, I pulled a muscle in the top of my right leg, and it was hurting for the rest of the day. This happened because I overworked it to compensate for my left side.

We then walked down to a park that had an activities/bushcraft centre. This centre was where we set up camp. Everyone was sharing a two-man tent and had foam roll mats, and I camped in luxury. I brought my own four-man tent, which I had to myself, and I also had an air-inflated floor mat. After my leg had hurt for half the day, it got quite bad when I could finally rest at camp: I struggled to get out of a chair, and I was all seized up. I then cooked pasta for my tea and realised I may not have brought enough food. Later that night, we made a fire until we went to bed.

The next day, we got up early, and I packed up. I was done before everyone else and helped them with their tents. It was then time for breakfast, which I didn't have because I was not hungry in the morning and never am really. Once we were ready to go, we got back in the minibus and went to a park full of deer. We parked a few miles away from the park and had to walk there and back on a trail. Just 10 minutes of walking and my leg was hurting again, but I didn't have to walk as far as I'd had to the day before, so it was alright. Halfway through walking, we stopped off at the park and ate some lunch. The night before, I realised I hadn't brought enough food, and all I had to eat to keep me going was a bag of Haribo. On the way back to the minibus, we took a wrong turn and had to double back on ourselves. When we got back to the minibus, we went back to where we had camped before we got dropped off at college. I helped unload the minibus while I waited for Graham to pick me up. That was the end of my expedition, and I had walked 17 miles in two days. I spent the next two days waiting for my right leg to get better.

After completing the exam and my walk for my Duke of Edinburgh, the rest of my time at college was finishing work off. I got all my work signed off by two teachers and just needed that third signature to leave for the summer. I found the teacher, and he said he couldn't sign me off because I needed to make changes to an assignment once it was marked. I came in the week after and made the changes I needed to. What I had to do next was produce an extra piece of work before I could leave. I did it that day and was then told that I needed to come back so I could print off all the evidence of my work, which I hadn't needed to do with my other teachers. I went in the week after that and printed my work off. I was then finally signed off and was off for the summer, which would give me a three-month break.

I had a few more lessons with my driving teacher at this point, and I thought that I was making very slow progress. My mum, on the other hand, wanted help with her own driving so went and got another driving teacher to help her. After her lesson with the other driving teacher, she recommended him if I wanted to change. Talk then shifted to my driving teacher trying to get as much money out of me as possible. After Graham opened my eyes to what was happening, I asked my driving teacher for the money back for the lessons that I had remaining. She did give me the money back but was trying to tell me how far I have come along to keep me as her student.

On my first lesson with the new driving teacher, he wanted to see where I was up to. He was shocked when I didn't use my mirrors, especially because I rode bikes. I just wasn't used to checking mirrors in a car. I didn't like the car straight away, and it took me a while to get used to it. I also told him that I booked a driving test on my birthday. I had booked it on my birthday because my previous teacher said that people were always forgetting which day their test was.

My second week off college was the final pool night of the season. On this particular night, we were away at a pub that was out of the area. Our team was in the top three of the league and winning that night may have got us a position higher in the league. Since I started going to the pool nights on Tuesdays, I was only watching and never played. A player did not turn up, so we were a player short. After the sixth game, the score was 3–3. The team needed an extra player to win on the night, so I was signed on for the last game of the season. I told my grandad that I was playing a game, and he was like a child excited to see me play.

A coin was flipped to see who had the pick to break. I guessed tails and got the pick. I let my opponent break, and the balls scattered, but nothing went down. I went to the table and potted two yellows before I missed. It was then my turn to wait, and I was shaking because I was so nervous. I went back to the table, and my nerves calmed when I was taking a shot. I potted a few more balls before I missed. He then potted a few more balls, and it was a black ball game. After taking turns trying to pot the last ball, it was lined up for me. I took my shot, and the black ball slowly rolled across the table and went into the pocket. Everyone on my team went crazy congratulating me, and someone even bought me a pint of Coke. It was a pint of Coke because I was on my motorbike. People who were not there were phoned up and told that I had won my first game. It wasn't just the first game that I won; I won the deciding game of the night. That was the end of the season, and many of the team said that they would leave at the end of the season. It looked like the end of the pool team at the pub, and I played the last game.

My dog Tisse was badly behaved at the start of 2022, so we went to an expert dog trainer. He was excellent and was able to get her to listen. He was teaching us how to treat the dog and how to correct her properly. He was doing this by walking Tisse round on a lead. As he trained gun dogs, Tisse would have to be on the left even though she was not going to be a gun dog. As he only trained dogs to walk on the left, you would have to hold the lead in your left hand. As I needed to hold the lead in my left hand a certain way, I found it difficult to do what this man was telling me. I even asked if I could switch hands because it would be easier. He said that that was not the right way to do it and I had to carry on doing it with my left hand. After trying and trying to do it with my left hand, I could see the man beginning to get frustrated. After I had my go doing it, my mum and Graham had their go, and it was over. He didn't want to have us back, and I think part of that was because I was struggling to do what he wanted with my left hand.

On 20th June, my sensei thought I was at a level that deserved recognition, and I earnt my first belt, which was red. Since I started karate, I had been going down in my own clothes and so had another person who joined at the same time as me. I then went to a martial arts shop and bought a gi, and I had to order a red belt online because they did not have them in my size. The next session that I went to, I received my certificate and had a couple of photos. After I got my red belt, I looked the part training at the dojo. Shortly after I got my first belt, I practised sparring with the basics that I had learnt.

It wasn't until this point that I tried adding kicks to my fighting repertoire. Everything that I had learnt and practised was punching and blocking with my arms. I had tried to kick before but never spent time practising; therefore, I was no good. When I had tried to kick previously, I was off balance and struggled to stay on my feet. This was nothing new because I have always struggled to balance on my left leg; I was only able to balance for two or three seconds before I fell over. It was for this reason that I was apprehensive about learning how to do kicks. I gave it a go, and with a little help, I surprised myself. I was doing better than I thought I would. When I first started, I had pins and needles in my right leg; with practice, they went away. I will admit that performing a kick is not my forte in karate, but I can adjust the kicks slightly for me to get the most use out of them. After practising for a few hours, my balance improved, and I can stay on my left leg for 10 plus seconds depending on what I am like that day.

At this point, I was 17 and without a job. I needed extra money, as the little money that I did get wasn't stretching far enough. For months and months, my gran was trying to persuade me to get a job. I wanted a job that I would like doing and didn't want to do just any job. That is why I decided to try and get a job at the start of the year, which didn't work out. It got to the point that my gran was treating me differently from my other brothers and sister. At that point, I thought the extra money would be nice. This was when I thought to go and see if I could get a job at the French restaurant called La Boheme my uncle worked at. What was the worst that could happen? The worst that would happen was them telling me I wasn't good enough and not to come back again.

I handed my CV in at the restaurant and didn't hear back for about two weeks. The captain of the pool team also worked at La Boheme and asked if I was still looking for a job. I told him that I was; he then gave me the number of the boss and told me to say to him that I was interested in working there.

One Wednesday night, I tagged along with someone and tried to do the job. There were only about 70 customers in. Even with this other person with me, I thought that was hard. The next day I struggled to walk and lost some more of the limited use in my hand because my left side is not used to being worked that hard. My left side was back to normal before my next shift.

On Saturdays, they have two pot washers because it is that busy. So, for the next few weeks, I did Saturday only to build up my confidence. I slowly got used to where all the plates and tubs went. I was then asked to do a weekday shift so I would be by myself. I was a bit hesitant, but I did it because I needed to do it if I was going to do it in the future. There were not that many people, so it was a good night to be by myself for the first time. I now do multiple shifts a week, so I am getting some money. It is not the best pay at six pounds per hour, but what do you expect for dishwashing?

The best part of being a dishwasher for me is that it is physical, but it is also a double-edged sword if I am not careful. Picking shot glasses up with my left hand and running around with a stack of heavy plates that I have to put away is hard work. At the time of writing this, I have worked here for two months, and my left side is getting stronger. This is because I am forced to use my left hand for hours a day. This has made my left hand more efficient; therefore, I am better at my job.

One of the improvements in my left hand that I have noticed is just as simple as holding a full pint glass. Before I started working at the restaurant, I could just about pick up an empty pint glass. Now I am able to hold a full pint glass if I need to. I still can't use it to carry a full drink, as my hand shakes, but I think that I could use it if I had a swig beforehand.

My uncle liked working at the restaurant because of the people who he worked with, and I can say the same as well. Everybody who works at the restaurant is nice, and there is one person in particular I get along well with – his name is Anthony. I have noticed that the people I get along with the most are substantially older than me, I've heard others with cerebral palsy are the same. Anthony is 60 years old and quite the character. We have similar interests. I ride a motorbike because I don't like cars, and he rides a push bike because he doesn't like cars. We both like camping, and he was interested when he heard about me writing a book, and he asks every week how it's going. Every day is a school day when I see him. Anthony was the main man that took me under his wing and looked after me and taught me how to do the job.

I want to thank the rest of the staff at the restaurant for giving me their helping hand when they see me struggling. I've noticed that they will even go out of their way to help me when my left side is affecting me more than normal. It would be a different job without all of you. One last thanks to the owners Adele and Olivier who have been disability friendly and allowed me to work at the restaurant. I would guess that other restaurants would not have wanted me to come back when I first started but they were very accommodating. I can use working at La Boheme as my physiotherapy and that is only possible because of them two. Oh, just one more thing, Adele tells everyone that I am her favourite.

At the start of August, I was thinking about what I could do to keep myself occupied when I was not at work or going to karate. I was struggling to go to sleep one night, and the idea of writing this book hit me. I thought if someone related to me and my experience, it would be good to show how I dealt with it. The next day, I just started writing and have been writing every day since.

My next big ride out was to the top of Anglesey. Me and my family were going to the farmer's field in our caravan for a few days. I had already decided that the next time I went away, I would go on my motorbike, if the weather permitted. I found my route on the A57 to the A56 and then got on the A55 around Chester until I got to the site. The night before I went, I took my bike to my grandad so my tyres were ready for the ride the following day. There were a few beers left, so I drank them before I went away. My mum thought that was a little stupid because of what I had to do the day after. I think it was just her fear of driving that was showing there.

On the day of the ride, I got geared up and set off an hour before the rest of them in the car. It was spitting where I lived, but 10 miles down the road, that cleared up. I got through Warrington and accidentally went on a side road to get on the A56. I didn't mind, though, as it was fresh tarmac on the country lanes that I went down to get on the A56. Going down that road, I was bouncing off my seat because the road was so bumpy. I was wearing my bag, and that caused my back to start aching. I got to Chester and went round on the A55. Riding at 70mph on a 125cc was impossible, so I tried my best to do 50 mph while trying not to labour my engine too much.

I missed the junction to carry on going to where I wanted to go, so I stopped off at Buckley. I went to the toilet and messaged my family, telling them where I was. I then got back on the road heading in the right direction. I was then going down this long road, and it was boring. The one thing that kept the trip interesting was pulling over to check on my chain. Ideally, the chain and sprocket needed to be replaced before I went, but AJS did not have the parts in stock.

I turned up to the field that we camp at, and my family were already there setting up the awning, which is almost like a conservatory for a caravan. They told me that they had only been there for 15 minutes, so I'd made it in good time. They also said that they saw me going the opposite way when I stopped off at Buckley. I looked at my chain, and it wasn't far from touching the floor. I wanted to leave Wales early because my brother wasn't getting along with Graham and my younger brother was fighting with my sister.

I went to Wales to relax, but I couldn't relax there, and my work offered me a shift the next day. I set off and got to the end of the road, and my brakes did not feel right and were not working as well as they should have. I then turned around and went back to the caravan. I did not want to risk going home with half-working brakes, so I stayed. Graham sorted my bike out for the next day when we were all going home.

I left early that day, as it was my mum's birthday, and her present was at my gran's; I wanted to get it wrapped so it would be ready for when she got back. On the way home, I felt paranoid about my bike not working properly, but then I got comfortable on it and rode back. So that I did not have to stop to go to the toilet, I did not have a drink until I got back. I had learnt my lesson coming back from Birmingham. I got to Menai Bridge, and there was a bigger bike next to me in the traffic. When the traffic cleared and split into two lanes, he shot off. Twenty minutes later, I rode past him while he was stopped at a bus stop. A few junctions before I got off, he then rode past me.

At the start of the journey, I found a truck and spent the majority of the trip behind him. He must have thought that I was following him until he got off at Chester, but I carried on. Towards the end, the sun was beating down on me, and I was very hot. This gave me a headache. I got back to my gran's house and sorted the present out and had breakfast and a nice cold drink.

Results day was 18th August 2022. I got an email the day before saying I could find my results online after 8.30am. I had completely forgotten about results day until I got that email. On results day, I woke up and tried to log on. The internet was not working at my house, so I rode up to college to get my results. I was in and out, no messing about. There was a sheet of paper saying that I got a distinction in my exam. Once I knew what I got, I wasn't bothered anymore and threw the piece of paper in the bin. I would have actually been somewhat surprised if I had got anything less than a distinction because of how easy I found the exam.

Later that day, the family went to the pub to play pool. I stayed an hour at the pub before I went to karate. At the end of the session, I was told by my sensei that they had brought the date of the next belt grading forward because of the progression that I had made since coming through the door and the dedication that I had shown in coming multiple times a week. I then went back to the pub and told my family what had happened. My mum said that a girl in the pub had got a distinction and two merits. The girl and the girl's mum were congratulating me on my distinction, but I was more impressed by the news that I had got while at karate. If anything, that day made me realise how chilled I am. I was told that the girl couldn't sleep the night before in anticipation, but if it wasn't for the email, I would have completely forgotten about results day.

The day after results day, I went back to my dojo for training. I arrived five minutes early, and one of my sensei was learning how to use the katana. He asked if I would like a go. I thought I would give it a try, and I was given a wooden sword. All I did was practise a downward slicing movement. It was at that point I found out that the weapons used in karate are harder to use than they look. I liked the idea of learning how to use a weapon, but the katana was not for me. The first reason that I joined karate in the first place was to use it as a form of rehabilitation. Keeping that in mind, I thought that the nunchucks would be a great way to exercise my left hand.

The next week, I asked if I could try the nunchucks. I was shown the basics and found out how hard they are to control. My first time using the nunchucks, I was practising with my right hand only. This was because I couldn't even use my left hand.

The next week, I practised them for a good length of time and was able to use my left hand to spin them round. I practise with these when I have the time and space to do so. Karate is the focus of my martial arts training, but using the nunchucks is an interest to me. They are not part of the main training I do but rather an extra that I practise in my own time.

It was time to go back to college, and I was looking forward to getting a regimented routine back. For weeks leading up to the first day back, I was wondering how many people had left the course. The first big change that I noticed straight away that day was we didn't have form in the mornings. I went to my old form tutor's room, and other people from last year were there, so I had gone to the right place. She told me that we didn't have form time anymore in the morning; rather, we had an hour of form on a Thursday morning. I was then given my timetable and found out that I was doing three half-days and one full day in college. I still had three days off, but my timetable didn't work well with the shifts at the restaurant I work at.

Throughout the day, I was expecting more people to come in late, but they didn't. There were only 10 people in my class who turned up. It had gone from 24 people to 10 in the space of a year. Thursday was the day where I could finish at 12pm, so I was home really early. Except complaining about my timetable, I didn't do much that day. It was on the news that the Queen died. I will always be able to remember when I went back to college for my second year, as it was the date of the Queen's death.

I wasn't in college long before I got tested for my yellow belt in karate. One day, I was at the dojo and we were lined up to go through the basics. I was putting my all into each kick, each punch and each block. I noticed that all the sensei were watching me and what I was doing. I had to make sure that I made no mistakes. After

15 minutes of going up and down the dojo, me and the other students could finally rest. Afterwards, the sensei told us that was part of our grade and that we had passed. As we moved on to practise for the next part of my grade, one sensei pulled me aside and told me if I had the same attitude with everything else that I did in life – like I do with karate – I would go far in life. Let's hope that is true and I can make it happen.

Another part of my grade was sparring. I practised and practised with my sensei – drilling a block and counterpunch. After weeks of practice, I did it with no mistakes. That was that ticked off for my grade.

The last and final part of my grade was rehearsing the katas I have been taught. I only needed to know two but knew part of the third. I did the first kata I have been doing since I joined, and I felt confident that I had done well. On my second kata, I announced the name and started to go through the third kata that I didn't even know that well. After the sensei quickly stopped me doing the wrong kata, I started again, and all was going well. That was until I turned and stumbled a little. I was annoyed that I stumbled, but I had another go of a kata of my choice. I had another go of the one where I stumbled to redeem myself. I thought that I did okay on that go, but I had to wait to find out.

At the end of the night, I was told that I had passed and received my certificate. Coming to the front to accept my certificate, I said, 'Cheers for that,' and shook the hands of all the sensei.

The first sensei shook my hand, pulled me in close and whispered, 'That is not how you accept an award,' but with a smile on his face.

My sensei, who is in charge of the dojo, has written a piece about me. Here it is:

This is basically an unbiased report on one of my students, Burt Rickman. Burt came to our Honbu Dojo to commence studying and training in the Japanese martial art of SHOTO RYU KARATE. I was made aware of his general disability by his mother and Burt himself. His physical problems soon became obvious to myself and co-instructors.

Burt had difficulties getting to grips with many of the basic techniques and applications, which are not easy for fully able-bodied students. In fact, a large percentage of practitioners never progress beyond these early stages due to the alien movements required for them to master in order to move forward from this preliminary stage. However, Burt was different. He applied himself wholeheartedly to learn and master these techniques, which was no easy task for him. His determination and attitude drove him forward and in quite short time, he adapted himself to competently perform the required techniques, and he satisfactorily gained his first senior grading, certified by the high Dan grading panel of the UK and Europe. Burt's physical improvement has continued, and he can now perform physical movement that previous to training was impossible for him. He continues to improve and has subsequently progressed to successfully pass his second-level senior grade. Burt's physical improvement is also matched by his growth in confidence both in the dojo classroom and in his activities in the outside world in general. Burt is a credit to our organisation and his family through his determination and fighting spirit to progress in martial arts and life. Professor Mike Lynch. 9th Dan Hanshi. Fellow of the International Guild of Masters.

It was around this time that I got contact lenses again. It is tedious taking your glasses off and putting them back on when you put your motorbike helmet on or take it off. The heavy use was also damaging my glasses because they were on and off my face so often. My gran and other people were also saying how much better I looked when I did not have my glasses on. Of course, that is what my gran would say, but she wasn't lying. This was all the persuasion that I needed. After a couple of weeks of wearing them, I was back up to speed putting them in and taking them out. In fact, my mum is amazed at my ability to take them out when I am so drunk I can't walk in a straight line. I have been wearing them every day since I got them again and haven't looked back.

For years, I have been told stories about the Oddballs Rally from my grandad. I went to the second Oddballs Rally of the year. While I was getting my gear ready, I forgot to bring a chair, and that was an inconvenience when camp was set up. I got to my grandad's house at 9am and didn't set off until 10.45am. The night before the rally, there was thick fog coming home from work, and I thought it wouldn't be good riding in this the following day.

When I woke up, there was about half of the fog from the night before. Decca and his Reliant Robin broke down before they even set off. He had a leak in the fuel line that he needed to fix. By the time he came round to my grandad's house, the fog had cleared, and it was a good ride out. When we got there, Decca left his trike at the entrance while we were signing in. There was a big queue of traffic waiting to get on the field. We met Terry there; he had been waiting there for us all morning. We got ourselves a brew, and my grandad topped it up with whisky. As Decca had left his trike out at the front, we had to get moving, and I burnt my mouth drinking my brew as quickly as I could. After setting up camp, I realised that I had forgotten to bring a chair and had to sit on Terry's trailer for the rest of the time there. We then went to the marquee and listened to the band until we called it a night.

I woke up multiple times throughout the night and finally got up at 8am when the crows in the forest next to the field wouldn't shut up. A husband and wife, both 80 years old – Mr and Mrs Oddballs, as my grandad calls them - came round and had a chat with us. They asked if we wanted to try some of this whisky and some of that whisky that they had on them. They were like a walking off-licence, with multiple flasks of different whisky that they were sharing.

Later that day, we had a look around at all the bikes that were there and were speaking to all the different people. We decided that we would have curry for tea. This is a brave move considering we only had porta-toilets. The curry turned out well and was quite tasty. After eating our tea, we went to the marquee early to get ourselves a table. That night, we decided to finish off all the beer that we had brought. Eight pints later, I had had enough for the night and went to bed. Shortly after, the rest of our group had the same idea and went to bed.

The next morning, I woke up at 8am and struggled to get out of my sleeping bag, and then I fell over getting out of the tent. I think I was still a little drunk from the night before. There was a thin layer of frost over the tent and all the bikes, as it was that cold that morning. My head was a little weary, but after two cups of tea, I was fine and putting the tent away. While we had a sit-down, we watched three people all trying to put away a pop-up tent. After 15 minutes (I would say), they got it away, and everybody watching cheered. It was about 10am when we were ready to go, and for some reason, I had to kick my bike for it to start. The village that we went through to get there was closed off, so we had to go via an alternative route home, which I quite enjoyed. I called in at my gran's, and she made me breakfast before I went home and put my gear away.

After I started working at the restaurant, I thought I would join the gym again. I thought about this for months, as I didn't want to go to work with the aches that you get when you first start going to the gym. This would make cleaning and putting plates away so much harder. One day, I decided that I was just going to do it anyway, so I went to the gym and got a membership. I was expecting to be sore the next day, but I wasn't. I went to the gym twice more that week but wasn't sore the day after. I then realised that pot washing is so physical that my body was already used to the extra stress. I had the idea of going to the gym for a couple of months but didn't want it to affect my ability at work as a consequence. Once I decided to go to the gym, I realised that I had wasted my time overthinking something that didn't even happen. I started going to the gym and did left-side work only to equalise both sides. That is a long process, and I am still doing it today.

After the pool season finished, we thought that was going to be the end because the players were moving to different teams instead. A few weeks before the winter season started, the landlord of the pub was getting a team together, and my name was on the sheet. He managed to find enough players for a full team. That meant that I was able to go out every Tuesday. The first week of the season, we were out of the area. It was near my college, the venue where I had to go to. I rode up on my bike after going to karate, and my grandad was having his game as I got there. It was a close match, and he didn't quite win it. It was then my game, and I didn't play as well as I thought I would because I wasn't practising enough.

Over the next few weeks, I went back to the pub to get more time on the table so I could at least stand half a chance of winning my next game. During my next game for the team, all was going well – I would even say that I had a slight lead. As soon as I gained that lead, I didn't know what day it was and made a mistake and gave the game away. At the start of the game, I was on yellows, and halfway through the game, I switched to reds and managed to pot one of my opponent's balls. He then had two shots, and the rest was history. I found it hard to win my games for the team, but I didn't stop turning up and trying my best each week to get the win.

I got in touch with my old friend Joel from cadets, who I hadn't spoken to in years, and we decided to meet in the pub. After a good night, he wanted to come again. I said that I would be in on Tuesday for the pool. When Tuesday came round, we were a player short, so we signed Joel on, and he played a good game. He then started coming every week after that.

At college, I did a unit on politics. I was given homework, which was to write a letter to my local MP about a problem that I was interested in. I thought that I would do an issue that I was genuinely interested in so I would be able to complete my homework and send it off to my MP to potentially fix. I asked my teacher whether I was allowed to write about the potholes that I had to ride over to get to college. He said I was, and so for the next two days, I thought about what I was going to put in the letter. After I came up with my points, I wrote them out. I said that the roads I went over to get to college were full of deep potholes and that they might cause an accident if left unattended. I then pointed out what I thought were the ones that needed to be fixed first. I then sent the letter to my teacher.

The deadline for the homework came round, and only me and two other people completed it. My teacher said he had already read my work and it was really well written. After I heard what my teacher thought of my letter, I sent it to my MP to see if the potholes would be filled in. Days went by, and I didn't get a reply.

My mum and Graham wanted to have a few days away, and out of all the places they could have gone to, they chose to go to Liverpool. To go away, they needed someone to look after my younger siblings. Who else better to look after them than me? I was asked to look after them, and I gladly agreed. The only problem was I had only looked after them for days at a time when they were off school. We figured out that I would be able to drop them off at school and pick them up for the first two days and would need my gran to drop them off at school on the last day. My mum dropped them off at school, and then it was my job to look after them. The first day was no bother; my mum even made tea for us on the first day.

The next day, I woke up and got Joe and May ready for school, then walked them there. I got back home and went to college. College finished, and I got back home. I then walked the dogs up to school to get Joe and May. When I picked Joe up, I asked him if he'd had a good day and if he'd behaved, and he convincingly said yes. As a treat on the way home, I let Joe and May go into the shop and buy some sweets.

When I got home, there was a toy that had finally been delivered after being ordered weeks ago. This was also a treat because Joe was behaving. I let him have it along with some of the sweets that he'd got himself. I then got a phone call asking how Joe was because he'd been naughty at school. My mum said that his teacher phoned her and said that Joe had refused to do work all morning and when he was told off, he had started copying what the teacher said. The best part was when his teacher told him that she would tell our mum how naughty he had been after school.

Joe said, 'You can't tell me off today because my big brother Burt is coming to pick me up.'

I couldn't even speak to his teacher to double-check because I was not allowed on the playground with my dogs. I seriously couldn't tell if he'd had a bad day at school that day. An hour after the phone call, I was making pasta from scratch, with Joe as my sous-chef.

The next morning, I got Joe and May ready, and my gran took them to school. She had to take them because I started college early that day. That was it – I didn't have to look after them after that. When I got home, my parents were back.

In the weeks leading up to my birthday and my driving test, I started having double driving lessons, and it made me realise that I had switched driving teachers just in time to have a decent chance of passing my driving test. My driving was good except for staying in the middle of my lane; I would steer slightly into the other lane when coming up to a roundabout. I went over the manoeuvres multiple times in preparation for my test.

One day, straight after work, I decided to go to the gym. My motorbike started just fine and got me to the gym. I spent an hour in the gym and went back to my motorbike. I turned the keys in the ignition, and there was no electricity. Without electricity, my motorbike won't start, even with a kickstart. After five minutes playing around with the ignition, I decided to call Graham and see whether it was a roadside fix. When he came, he looked at the battery and some fuses to see if they were the problem. There was nothing that Graham could do, so I had to push my bike home from the gym after being at work all day. I gave my helmet and jacket to Graham to take home.

I crossed the road with my bike, and my biological dad was pulling out of the road where he lived opposite the gym. This was the first time that I had physically had contact with him in a while and the first time that I had spoken to him in seven years. He got out of his van and said that he would have dropped me and my bike off home, but his van was full to the rafters. He then asked me where my jacket and helmet were and whether I needed them to be taken home. For the next part to make sense, keep in mind that Graham is my dad in my eyes, so that is what I call him.

When my biological dad asked if I needed anything to be taken home, I said, 'Don't worry. My dad (Graham) is taking them back in the car.'

After a short conversation with my biological dad at his van, I started to push my bike home. Immediately after I started moving, Graham pulled up at the bus stop adjacent to my dad's van and asked whether I was going to get a lift home with this bloke. He was oblivious that the man with the van was my biological dad. I then pushed my motorbike home thinking that you couldn't write what happened, but here I am writing it into my book.

As part of my government policies unit at college, my teacher arranged to go to London for a day to see Parliament. The week leading up to going to London, I could see that the potholes that I had addressed in my letter to my MP were filled in. I thought it may have been a coincidence. I no longer had to dodge the potholes in the roads like mines in a minefield.

When we went to London I arranged to leave my motorbike at my friend's house, as I didn't want to leave it in the middle of Manchester. The train left Manchester at 6.15am, so to get there in time, I had to wake up at 4.30am. I was half-asleep until I got out of the house because it was a sub-zero temperature; there was ice all over the family car. It was just lucky that there was no rain on the road that turned to ice.

I got on my bike and rode over to my friend's house. On the way there, it was so cold that my teeth were chattering. I got to his road, went past his house and then saw my friend running down the street after me. After I got to the right house, I went down the alley to his back garden. My friend and his dad helped me get my bike over the step into the garden. I didn't bring a coat because I didn't need one, but my friend's mum gave me a jacket that stayed in my bag the entire day. His mum then dropped us off at Piccadilly station with time to spare.

The train journey there and back was between two and two and a half hours each way, and I wasn't going to waste that time doing nothing. I brought my laptop so I could spend that time writing this book. Not many people knew that I was writing a book until this point, and a couple of them were interested and wanted to read what I had done. Poppy stole my laptop from me while I was in the middle of reading what I had written. I only got my laptop back when Caitlin told her to give it back to me.

When we arrived, we waited at the train station to get the tickets to go on the underground. One thing that I noticed straight away was how quickly people were walking. Some people weren't actually far from jogging. I couldn't get my head around why people were rushing to get to their jobs. We all then went on the underground to get to the Houses of Parliament. When we got there, I didn't even know where I was. We had a guided tour around Parliament, and I was amazed by the size of the place and all the artwork inside; there was a lot of attention to detail. The point of the tour was to go and physically see what we had been learning about in class.

After the tour, we went into a room where we had the chance to listen to Lord Balfe and his experiences in politics. It was fascinating to hear his stories and his thoughts about certain people. He told us what he had achieved and gave me a better insight into how Parliament works.

By this time, it was lunch, and I'd only had a light breakfast, so we went to get food. I am not a picky eater, but I like to only eat healthy food, and if there isn't any, I won't eat. Everyone else who went to London wanted to go to McDonald's. I do not eat McDonald's, and there was a Sainsbury's next door. There was nothing in there that I wanted to eat either, so I went hungry until I got food at home.

After we finished eating, we were supposed to go to the Churchill War Rooms museum, but as we were running out of time, we wandered around London instead. We went to Buckingham Palace and all along the Thames. We also visited government buildings. We were hopping on and off the underground everywhere, and I thought that the transport in London was fantastic. I found it funny that there were queues to take a picture in front of a red phone box. Overall, I thought that it was good to go to London, but the only thing that I didn't like was how many people were there and how many people would walk into me if I didn't move out of the way.

When we had finished sightseeing, it was time to get back on the train. We were in a rush to get there and made it on time. I then chilled out on the train until we set off. Poppy sat next to me on the way home because she wanted to help me write this book – at least she didn't steal my laptop again. For some reason, it felt like it took longer to get home than it did to get to London.

We got back to Manchester and had to make our own way home. I didn't know how to get back, and if I hadn't gone home with my friend, I would still be at Piccadilly station now. We got to the bus stop, and it started raining. I forgot about the coat in my bag, and I was soaked. It didn't bother me, though, because I am a biker. It took ages to get back. I then had to get my bike gear on and carefully get my bike out of the back garden. Apparently, my friend's sister freaked out when she saw my bike in the garden because their family are against riding motorbikes. I then made my way home in the wet night and dodged cars that were out to get me. By the time I got home, it was 8.30pm, and I had been out all day. I then had my tea.

My mum said that a letter had been delivered to me. I opened it up, and it was a letter from my MP saying that she had contacted the council to fill in the potholes that I mentioned. It wasn't just a coincidence that the road was fixed where I had pointed out. I then collapsed into bed.

It was getting close to my birthday and my driving test. I wanted to pass my driving test to get it out of the way and have my licence, but I had to wait and see what would happen on the day. I didn't even want to get a car, but I thought it couldn't hurt to get my licence.

The day before my birthday and test, I was coming home from college on my motorbike, and the traffic was at a standstill on the dual carriageway. I decided to filter through the middle of all the traffic to get home. Five minutes went by, and I managed to squeeze through the gaps and nearly got in front of all the traffic. A gap between a car and a bus closed, so I had to stop, and I lost my balance because of my left side. I put my feet down, and the bus ran over my left foot. I was in agony for five minutes, and I stayed in the traffic while I waited for my foot to feel better. I still had to use it to change the gears. I wondered whether to go to hospital or not, but after 10 minutes, it calmed down, and I went to the gym before I went home. I was meant to be going to karate and was annoyed that I had hurt my foot. I still thought about going to karate because I didn't want to miss a session.

When I got back, my foot was a mess – all bruised and swollen – but I didn't think I had broken anything. My mum freaked out when she got home because Graham said I had been hit by a bus. After she realised it wasn't that bad, she started thinking about my driving test booked for the next morning. I just hoped I would be able to take my test.

The next day, I woke up and had an hour before my driving teacher picked me up. It was my 18th birthday, and so I opened a couple of presents while I waited to be picked up. My biological dad got me a card and some cake. After my foot had been run over by a bus, my nail was coming off, so I found a few of my sister's dinosaur plasters and used them. I had to squeeze my foot into my shoe, which was a struggle because my foot was that swollen. I got in the car and drove down to the test centre without much pain. We then went over some questions before it was time for my test.

As I started my test, all was well, and I told my examiner it was my birthday. I didn't mind doing my test, and I thought that I was doing alright. I came up to a roundabout and got in the wrong lane; I didn't follow the lane because I would have ended up on the motorway. That was the first place that I failed. The next place where I failed was turning right off a main road, stopping quickly and ending up a little past the junction. I knew when I did that I would be marked down but didn't think it would mean I'd fail my test. One other thing that happened was that my left hand was struggling to use the gears a little, but it was nothing terrible. During my test, I forgot about my foot, and it didn't affect my driving. I got back to the test centre and was told that I had failed, but I wasn't bothered in the slightest because I still had a motorbike. It was only on the way home that I told my driving teacher that I had been run over by a bus the day before. He wasn't bothered because I was still able to take my test but did say I was the type of person who would get run over by a person. When I got back home, I told my parents that I failed, and that was that.

I then took my dogs for a walk and called at my gran's on the way home. When I got there, I was only allowed in the front room but didn't think anything of it. It was so I couldn't see the buffet that my gran was making for my surprise party at the pub later that night. I wanted to go to the pub for my birthday and have a few drinks but didn't want to make a big deal of it.

When I got back, I got ready and went to the pub early. When I arrived, there were birthday banners at the bar and balloons everywhere. It took me a good minute to realise what was going on. I was confused as to why Decca and Jarvo were there. When I cottoned on to what was happening, everyone asked to buy me a drink, and I drank John Smith's that night. I got on the pool table and was playing terribly.

After three games, I had a break and was talking to everyone. Not many people were there, but the ones who were there, I knew well. Joel came later and got me a pint. At first, I had my pints stacking up at the bar because I wasn't drinking fast enough, so I had to pick up the pace.

At the end of the night (when I was wasted), I started playing pool again and somehow got better. I was struggling to walk around the table, but I was able to win the games. After a few games against Joel and Graham, I walked home. After I got in, I couldn't remember what had happened, but I fell asleep on the toilet. I woke up in the middle of the night, threw up everywhere in the bathroom and got into my own bed.

The rest is yet to be written

What you have just read are my most memorable moments from being born to my first day as an adult. In this chapter, I want to share what I have learnt from writing about my life in this book. I will also give you an idea of what I want to do in the future.

The first lesson that I have learnt from writing this book is that you should always try new things, even if you think it is going to be difficult. This is because you might surprise yourself and do better than you thought you would. On the other hand, you could try something new and struggle doing it. At least you will know that you struggle doing it. I guess it comes down to: you don't know if you don't try. I relate this to not working at the restaurant when I was 16, as I thought I would not be able to do the job. I only started working at the restaurant when I needed the extra money, and I surprised myself at how I handled my first shift.

The next lesson I have learnt is that every cloud has a silver lining. If you look hard enough at your problem, you will find the positives. I think that most of my work ethic comes from the fact that I had to spend years learning how to walk and then spend years catching up on my schoolwork. The silver lining may be as simple as being able to bring someone to talk to when you go fishing. Take the most that you can out of a situation.

Another lesson that I have learnt is to be thankful for your situation and realise that it isn't too bad. Whatever your problem is, just remember that there is someone in the world who has it worse than you. Be thankful for what you do have and imagine what your life would be like if you didn't have it.

If there is an activity or hobby that you like doing but can't see a reason to carry on doing anymore, find another one. I have to always be working towards something for me to do something. I have always been interested in music and tried many different instruments. When I quit the Air Cadets, I wish that I had found the local brass band or something similar so I would have carried on playing the trumpet. Don't stop doing what you enjoy.

If you are trying to achieve a goal, don't stop trying; keep practising, and over time, you will get there. There is no such word as 'can't', and with enough time and practice, you can achieve anything. People take pride in different achievements depending on how hard it is to get them and how long it has taken them.

The penultimate lesson that I have realised from writing my book is that being successful and being 'a nobody' starts with the mind. If you believe, then you can; if you don't believe, then you can't. My parents are the key to my success because they have always thought I should try anything and everything while pushing me to be independent. I sometimes think if my parents didn't use tough love, how different my life would be different? Would I set limits for myself, and what skills would I not have that I currently do?

The last lesson that this book has highlighted to me is that you have to play the cards that you are dealt and make the best hand possible. There is no point wishing that your cards are different, as they can't change. Rather, try your best to make the most out of the cards that you have. If you do that, then you know you are making the best out of your life.

In the near future, I can see myself either at university or in a job working for customs and excise. I will try to get my car licence and also get my next bike licence. I want to go to the Elephant bike rally in Germany.

In five years' time, I can see my hobbies paying off. I can see myself having a black belt in karate, and I can also see myself being in a band. I can see myself visiting Italy. I can also see myself taking part in a major sports event, but I don't know which one. Lastly, I can see myself trying my best to inspire others to be the best that they can be.

I know what you might be thinking: am I gay? No. Even though I have had interest from a few girls and it didn't go any further, I am not bothered whether I have a girlfriend or not. My family and my progress are more important to me. It doesn't help that I am near clueless in knowing if girls like me or not. The day will come when I get myself a girlfriend, but who knows when that will be? If you are interested and are free between 12pm and 2pm every week on a Friday, then do not hesitate to message me.

I think it would be nice someday to sit down and have a conversation with my biological dad, but I don't feel the need to yet. I probably should speak to him but, for me, Graham has filled the gap that he left. Having said that, I would not exist without my dad, and for that, I have to thank him. I'll have to wait and see how the future unfolds.

I am happy in life with what I have achieved so far and have plans for the future. One of my plans was to write this book and get people to read it. If you have read this book to the end, I think that is a success. I hope you enjoyed reading this book and it helped you in some way. To be continued?

Printed in Great Britain
by Amazon

30668827R10077